Valleywood

THE AUTOBIOGRAPHY OF
LATEYSHA GRACE

JOHN BLAKE

Published by John Blake Publishing Ltd,
3 Bramber Court, 2 Bramber Road,
London W14 9PB, England

www.johnblakepublishing.co.uk

www.facebook.com/johnblakebooks ⬛
twitter.com/jblakebooks ⬛

This edition published in hardback in 2015

ISBN: 978 1 78418 269 4

British Library Cataloguing-in-Publication Data:

A catalogue record for this book is available from the British Library.

Design by www.envydesign.co.uk

Printed in Great Britain by CPI Group (UK) Ltd

1 3 5 7 9 10 8 6 4 2

Papers used by John Blake Publishing are natural, recyclable products made
from wood grown in sustainable forests. The manufacturing processes conform to
the environmental regulations of the country of origin.

Every attempt has been made to contact the relevant copyright-holders,
but some were unobtainable. We would be grateful if the appropriate people could
contact us.

For Mum, the strongest person I've ever known.
I love you very much.

CONTENTS

PROLOGUE

In school, I was always the class clown. Up dancing, carrying on, being the centre of attention – that was me. You could say I've always aspired to become famous, given all the attention I craved. I kind of knew that I would be famous someday too, but for the time being I was stuck in secondary school, completely directionless.

When I was in sixth form I was the cockiest girl in my year, especially when it came to the male teachers. I would deliberately cross the line between friendly and flirting. I'd call out to them from down the corridor and say something along the lines of 'Morning, Mr Thompson, have you been working out?' in an overtly girlie manner, twisting my hair round my finger as I said it, or maybe giving them a pout of my lips.

Seeing them grow uncomfortable made me smile to myself. I had absolutely no interest in any of my teachers, romantic or otherwise; I just loved the way I could make them blush.

During school I set my own rules: turned up when I wanted, went home when I got bored and behaved how I saw fit. Other rules and regulations didn't apply to me, it was almost as if I thought I was a cut above my peers. My teachers did all they could to try and engage me while I was there, but in the end they just gave up trying. Every time they thought they were making headway with me, I would skip school again and be back to square one. I can't blame them for being so frustrated. I used to see it on their faces when they screamed at me – they were at the end of their tether. Maybe I should have paid more attention, not because I would change anything about my life now, but because I'll never get the opportunity to learn like that ever again.

But when I was there, my mind was never on my work; I didn't have the attention span to sit still and learn. It's almost as if I had ADHD (Attention Deficit Hyperactivity Disorder), but I was never diagnosed. I'm still the same today. You can tell me something and five minutes later, I'll forget we've ever spoken. If you can hold my attention for more than ten minutes, you're doing well!

So when I was expelled from school in 2009, I was secretly delighted. Honestly, I could have done cartwheels when I knew I didn't have to go back to that hellhole. I'm sure most kids would regard being kicked out of school as unthinkable, but I've never been the academic, play-by-the-rules kind of girl. For me it was a blessing in disguise.

So, how did I get expelled, I hear you ask. Well, it happened one lunchtime when I was seventeen and in the Upper Sixth at St Joseph's Catholic Comprehensive school, in the coastal town of Port Talbot. My mates and me were chilling in the common room, like we always did. We had some hot boys in my year, but none so lush as a guy called Andrea. He was of Greek origin and looked as if he might have hailed straight from the Gods. An absolutely gorgeous guy, he was one of the most popular lads in our school.

I don't know how it all came about, but one of my friends

thought it would be hilarious to dare me to give him a lap dance. I'm not the type of girl to turn down such a challenge, so I sashayed over to him, pushed his pals out of my way and told him what he was about to witness. Andrea smiled, rocked back on his chair and said, 'Bring it on!'

My friend Casey turned the common room CD player on and out blasted Beyoncé's 'Crazy In Love'. It's one of my all-time favourite songs and I love dancing to it.

Imagine the scene… in came that big, booming infamous beat as I started doing a lap round Andrea's chair and playing with the back of his hair.

'Yes! So crazy right now,' said Jay-Z, as I began winding and grinding my hips in time to the music.

'Most incredibly it's your girl B,' I mouthed, giving my best chest wiggle to the crowd.

Singing along in time to the lyrics and flicking my locks back like a complete diva, I felt alive. Everyone in the common room was uniformly appreciative and started to form a circle around Andrea and me. They were cheering 'Go on Lateysha!' as my routine began to get saucier. On I continued, 'Lookin' so crazy, your love's got me lookin'. Got me lookin' so crazy your love…'

My uniform was the most unsexy thing you could imagine but I was doing the best I could with what I had to work with: a pair of black trousers, a white shirt, a sickly coloured yellow, green and red tie, plus a black blazer emblazoned with the school crest.

As the music continued to blast out from the speakers, I took my tie off in a seductive manner and wrapped it around Andrea's neck, pulling him closer into me. Then I turned myself away from him and shimmied my blazer down my back before casting it away on the floor.

By this time all the lads and girls couldn't believe what they were seeing. They started heckling and cheering like it was Queen Bee herself giving a concert in the school. 'Work it Teesh,' I remember one crying, and another screamed, 'Shake that booty, baby!' The room was electric with excitement. I started to shake my ass in his face, while slowly unbuttoning my school shirt. When I think back, I can't actually believe it. Christ, I had no shame!

I carried on singing the lyrics while I spun round and undid the last few remaining buttons, until my red satin New Look bra was on show. As sexily as I could, I peeled off my shirt and the room just erupted. Now, I was only wearing black school trousers, my 70-denier tights, sappy school shoes and the ruby red bra.

The noise was getting louder and louder. So loud, in fact, a teacher about three hundred yards away came storming into the common room to see what all the fuss was about. He must have thought a fight had broken out because it wasn't uncommon in our school for two pupils to go at it with each other. I remember I was wiggling my hips when I heard a voice bellow, 'What on EARTH is going on in here?'

The crowd dispersed slightly and when he spotted me stripping off for one of my fellow pupils, he screamed my name in complete horror, 'LATEYSHA!'

The room fell silent as I turned around and saw Mr Callas in complete shock. It was as if time stood still and suddenly I was very aware I was wearing only my bra and school pants in front of the head teacher. It was as if I couldn't move. My mouth was wide open and I just froze out of fear, like a rabbit in the headlights. I didn't know what to do next.

'Turn that music off RIGHT NOW!' he shrieked and spluttered, pointing to the CD player in the corner of the room.

No longer could Jay-Z's rapping and Beyoncé's belting tune be heard.

Honestly, I've never seen a man so angry in my life. He couldn't even form the words properly in his mouth, he was that furious.

'Put some clothes on!' he shouted, turning his head away and trying not to look at my underwear, which was on full display.

I waded through the hoards of teenagers, holding my boobs into my bra while I looked for my shirt and blazer on the floor.

'All of you GET OUTSIDE!' he screamed at the crowd. 'Lateysha, you get to my office NOW!' His face had turned a bright purple colour and a vein in his head was bulging.

Andrea just looked at me and laughed. So, why wasn't he being reprimanded as I was? I didn't know what was coming my way, but I knew it wasn't going to be good.

Once I had got dressed, I was immediately marched by Mr Callas down to his office. His secretary had been instructed to phone my mother and he made me wait in the corridor until she arrived.

When she turned up, she was all flustered and didn't know why she had been called in so abruptly. They hadn't told her what I'd done; they just said she needed to come to the school as soon as possible. At first she thought it must have been something to do with my behaviour or lack of attendance – some days it was a miracle I turned up for any lessons at all. My mum asked me what was going on and I couldn't form the words in my mouth quick enough before Mr Callas called us both into his office.

He asked my mother to take a seat, while he made me stand at the edge of his desk. I was obviously that disgusting to him, I wasn't even allowed to sit on his battered leather chair.

'Mrs Rigdon,' he began, clearing his throat. 'This lunchtime, I witnessed your daughter exposing herself to a fellow colleague in the common room.'

I rolled my eyes and smirked because he was making this sound far worse than it was. Exposing myself? Like I was some kind of pervert and I was shoving my boobs in Andrea's face against his will.

He must have caught my facial expression because after that he began to unload on me right in front of my mother.

'What on EARTH are you laughing at, Lateysha?' he yelled. 'In ALL my years of teaching, I have NEVER seen anything so tawdry in all my LIFE! I have NEVER seen such DISGRACEFUL behaviour from any pupil in thirty years and you think this is FUNNY?'

His voice got louder and increasingly angry the more he spoke. My heart was racing; I could literally feel it thumping in my chest.

'I just cannot BELIEVE what I saw this afternoon. I'm still in complete shock!' he continued.

Meanwhile, my mother looked completely confused. It seemed she didn't know what to say or where to look.

'Mum,' I told her, 'it's not as bad as it sounds! I was dared to do a striptease for one of the lads in the common room and I thought it would be a laugh.'

'A LAUGH?' Mr Callas interjected irately.

'I didn't expose any part of myself. I had a bra on,' I carried on, explaining to her in an effort to limit the damage.

'Well, who knows how far you would have got if I hadn't walked in on you?' Mr Callas shouted. 'This is just the tip of the iceberg, Lateysha. Your grades are poor, you walk around like you own the place, you are cocky, you distract all the other pupils, your attendance is pathetic, you are rude to staff. Your homework is never done on time and quite frankly, we don't want you at this school any longer!'

My mum was quiet. She looked at me with venom in her eyes. I knew she was angry and embarrassed I'd put her in this situation but she didn't know what to say because everything he had said was true. She was absolutely mortified.

In the end she said very little, apart from promising the headteacher I would change my ways. 'I'm sure if I have a talk with her, I can get her to start behaving,' Mum pleaded. 'If you throw her out of school, what hope will she have?'

But nothing she said could have changed his mind. He was adamant I was too disruptive for the other pupils. 'It's too little too late, Mrs Rigdon. I cannot continue with her antics, it affects all the other students,' he said, and kicked me out of school that very afternoon. I was never to return to St Joseph's again; I wasn't allowed to say goodbye to my friends or teachers. I was to pack up my locker and leave with immediate effect.

When he told me I was kicked out, I just stood there at the end of his desk, staring him down with so much attitude, I think he was scared of me. But he meant nothing to me and neither did his poxy school. The fact he'd just expelled me had no impact – I didn't care, I *hated* the place! I didn't even see it as a punishment. Looking back now, I can't believe what I did. It was so reckless and I had effectively thrown away a good future. Luckily, things have worked out well for me, but I would never advise anyone to do what I did. Your school days really are the best days of your life, cherish them while you can because, believe you me, it's a big bad world out there and you will regret not paying attention when you had the chance.

My mother shook the headteacher's hand when she left, which made me angry. For all I knew, this guy had just shattered my future and she was *thanking* him for it. I couldn't believe it. Whose side was she on, anyway?

She had been quiet in Mr Callas's office, but as we walked home she certainly became vocal and physical about how she felt.

'What the fuck are you going to do now, Lateysha?' she wailed, slapping me on the back of the head. 'I am not having you hanging around the house all day. As soon as you get home, you better find another college!'

I knew she was seriously mad if she was cursing and walloping me. She very rarely felt the need to give me a slap, but then again it wasn't every day I got expelled from school. And it wasn't very hard, it's not like she was full on digging me out or anything.

'Mum, calm down, I'll sort something out,' I told her.

'You better, Lateysha, because I'm not going to look after you. You got yourself into this mess, you can get yourself out of it!' she screamed as she struck me again.

'Fine, I will. I will join somewhere else,' I moaned, just wanting her to shut up about it.

'I can't believe you would strip in front of all your classmates. What the fuck were you thinking, behaving like that?' she yelled as she cracked me again.

'It was just a dare, Mr Callas has taken it all out of context.'

'I can't believe it! Now you will have no qualifications. What are you going to do with your life?' she said, shaking her head in sheer disbelief.

There was a long pause before I smiled and said, 'I don't know, become a stripper?'

INTRODUCTION

Most of you will know me from the MTV show *The Valleys*, which sadly came to an end in 2014. We had three hilarious seasons that showcased my fellow housemates and me as we were plucked from obscurity and given the chance to make something of ourselves in the Welsh city of Cardiff. I always had ambitions of being on TV, so when I heard about *The Valleys* I jumped at the chance to be part of a new, exciting project. As I had nothing to lose, I threw caution to the wind and gave the show my all.

I like to look back on my time on the programme with fond memories and you can trust me when I say I was devastated when it all came to an end. When you are virtually talentless and picked to become part of a reality series for sheer shock factor, the fame you inherit can be snatched away just as easily as you were given it, I suppose. But hey, that's showbiz. One day you're hot, the next day you're not. Fame is fickle, my friend, always remember that.

The Valleys was the vehicle that launched my media career, but let me tell you now it hasn't defined me as a person. Since I first hit the screen in 2012 I have forged a good spell in the limelight by presenting TV shows, I've had success with a couple of hit singles, performed in music videos, done countless magazine interviews and travelled around the world, meeting fans on PAs (personal appearances).

From all that, people think they automatically know me – but you only see what I allow you to see. Believe me when I say there's much more to me than meets the eye. A very select few really know me, and where I've come from. These people are my friends and family, who have been there guiding me through some of the most traumatic times any person can go through in life. Without them and their compassion, who knows where I'd be, if still here at all.

No one has given me a handout along the way. I've worked super-hard to get where I am today and while I may still be small fry compared to many celebrities on the circuit, I'm willing to graft harder than anyone else to make sure I continue to be propelled up the ladder.

But enough of the introduction…

Since you've bought this book, I'm guessing you must want to get to know me a little better. So, who exactly is Lateysha Grace and where did she come from, right?

Well, sit back, relax and get ready for what you're about to read. I don't do anything by halves and when I agreed to write this 'warts and all' account of my life it was on the condition that I could say what I want, how I want and in the way I want. There will be no teams of production crews editing me out, no journalists sifting through to find the best quote. And no pesky parents telling me to calm down and be a better role model.

I know some people tailor their life stories for particular audiences, but you won't get that from me. In my opinion honesty is better than sugar-coated bullshit, so don't judge me for being truthful, because this is my life so far: from the valleys to 'Valleywood'.

Chapter One

BACK TO THE
OLD SKOOL

In the words of my idol Beyoncé 'let's take it from the top' and start at the very beginning of my humble story. The Lateysha you all know and love was born to my mother, Deborah Grace, and my estranged father, Leroy Henry, on 25 November 1992. I was officially named Lateysha Naomi Henry, but as you will come to read I've had some troubling times with my father and so I decided to use the name Lateysha Grace instead, to honour my mother.

Why my mum was ever interested in my dad is beyond me, but I understand she was only twenty and very naïve when she first met him. Originally from Port Talbot, Mum moved to Birmingham one summer for work. She was working in a jeweller's and had been having a few drinks in a pub called Rosie O'Grady's when my dad took a shine to her.

Mum has always been a good-looking girl. Long brown hair, sexy green eyes, a button nose and a petite frame ensured she was never short of male attention. As the story goes, she was strutting

1

her stuff on the way out of the bar when out the corner of her eye she saw this car slow down. Leroy was so taken with this beautiful young woman he approached her and asked for her number. My mum was flattered, as any woman would be, and after Leroy had worked his charm on her, she agreed to give him her digits. Just like that. A few days later he took her out on a date and it all happened from there, very quickly. When I think about it now, a man with that kind of confidence is usually a player; they will try their luck with all sorts of girls. For those guys, picking up chicks is like firing loads of bullets; in the end you are bound to get one or two targets.

When my mum and Leroy got together he already had two kids with another woman, a fact that surely ought to have set alarm bells ringing in Mum's head, but it didn't. I guess she fell for him and his smarming pretty hard. Mum met his kids a few times and did her best to be cool with the situation until one day, when she found a note pushed through her door with photos attached. It seemed another woman was claiming to have had a child with my dad and he was refusing to believe it was his. This other lady had tried to get in contact with Leroy many times, but for whatever reason he didn't want to know her and wasn't there for his new son. Probably because he had someone else occupying his time now – my mum.

I couldn't say they were love's young dream or anything because all I ever hear from anybody is that they weren't in a very good relationship. My mum says Leroy wasn't very trustworthy: he was sneaky with his phone and his movements, which made her wary of him and meant she could never fully believe what he said to her. But despite turbulent times just a few months after they had met, she fell pregnant with me. The situation wasn't ideal, but at no point did Leroy ever say he wouldn't support her, so she agreed to keep me despite being only a tender twenty-year-old and earning a pitiful wage.

Five months into the pregnancy, Mum finally realised Leroy was a useless waste of space because he was cheating on her with other women and sleeping around. One night, after they had had yet another blazing row, she made the tough decision to leave him and move back to Neath, South Wales, to live with her dad, my Grandpa Michael. My grandma had moved away when they separated.

Upping sticks like that mid-pregnancy was daunting. Times were tough for Mum, her whole world had been turned completely upside down. Now she had no job, no boyfriend, no money, no fixed address; in other words, no stability. She once told me she would wake up every day panicked about the future and because of this she became terribly anxious and deeply depressed. Hearing all this as an adult saddens me beyond belief. I can just imagine my young mum being scared and alone. And not enough credit goes to these women. No one goes out there wishing to be a single mother, but sometimes it happens because men decide not to be fathers.

When she finally went into labour with me, she had virtually no one around for support and in the end she had to call one of her old friends to coach her through the birth. By all accounts it was a dreadful delivery; for a full twenty-four hours Mum was in screaming labour, until eventually out I popped into the world.

When the nurse handed me over to my exhausted mother, Mum says she looked down at me and couldn't quite believe how ugly I was! After all that agony she had just been through, this hideous baby was the result of the pain and suffering. I had no hair, I was all crinkled up, with a huge head, and weighing in at a pretty hefty 8lb 13oz. We have a laugh about it now but when she tells me

I looked like a little gargoyle, I don't believe her. I categorically refuse to think I was anything but a cherub.

After my birth, my father Leroy had very little to do with me. In fact, the first time he saw me, at four months old, he was convinced I was a white baby and completely denied I was his. It wasn't until I was a little older, around eight months, when my skin began to darken, he turned round and said, 'Ah, now she looks a lot like my son.' To this day, I don't think he even apologised to my mum for saying I wasn't his. Cheap shot, if you ask me.

Mum didn't take to motherhood like some women do and even though she loved me she admits bringing me up was extremely difficult for her. I think a lot of it was down to her situation. She was still living with her dad at the time, but they had a very strained relationship. He wasn't happy about my mum having a baby so young and distanced himself from her, despite them living together. It must have been awful for Mum. She had literally no one to help her out, financially or emotionally. I can't begin to imagine how challenging life must have been for her back then.

Mum kept in contact with my dad and updated him on how I was when I was younger, whether he wanted to know or not. But it wasn't until I was about four that my warring parents decided to mend some bridges. Mum arranged for me to be babysat by my auntie Paula, so she could go to Birmingham to see Leroy. She says her reasons for going were so she could make peace with him, build a relationship and, hopefully, make my life easier. Even though he had so far been a disinterested douche, Mum didn't want me to grow up never knowing anything about my real father, so you can't blame her for wanting to go and visit.

Incredibly, when my mum and dad met up again they got on like a house on fire. Gone were all the arguments and ill feelings. Instead they spent the whole night chatting about me and how I was growing up so fast. The undeniable chemistry and Leroy's unfailing charm, which had been there when they first met, was back. I suppose you could say one thing led to another and you've guessed it, they slept together again.

Leroy must have some pretty powerful swimmers because that one night of wild passion led to my brother Regan being conceived. Mum was stunned. It's not like she planned to get pregnant, but she reasoned that she and Leroy had got on so well that evening, maybe there could be a future. But come on, let's be honest – Leroy already had four kids he wasn't bothered about, so why would he care now?

At first to me the idea of having a new baby brother was unthinkable. I didn't want to be vying for my mum's attention and competing for her affections with another child. But as soon as Regan was born, in December 1996, I was totally smitten. I loved him more than I could ever have imagined and today we have an unbreakable bond that no one can deny.

Like I said, things never worked out with Leroy and Mum despite her now having two children with him. She tried her best to involve him in our lives but he wasn't interested. Not that it bothered me – I didn't care because I didn't know any different. But I remember Mum crying over the rejection many times and she became very depressed and miserable. She never envisaged this was how her life was going to be; when Leroy said he would support her, she believed him. All her future dreams had been shattered, so I guess she was allowed to be depressed. Had it been me I wouldn't have been able to cope at all. My mum doesn't really like speaking about that time much because it brings back many bad memories. She's told me in the past she 'wished my upbringing had been better', but she was so sick at the time. Depression is a horrible illness, and just because you can't see it doesn't mean it should be taken any less seriously than something like self-harming.

No kid ever wants to see their mum upset and some of my earliest memories revolve around her tears, which in itself says a lot about my childhood. But back then, to be honest, I preferred it that Leroy was out of the picture. We didn't need him, we would be absolutely fine, just Mum, Regan and me – they were my whole world.

If only it could have stayed that way.

Chapter Two
NEW DAD

As you've probably guessed, times changed fairly quickly after Regan was born and even though I was selfishly content with our little family trio, my mum wasn't. Don't forget she was still a young woman, only twenty-six, with two small kids to look after. She's never been one of those downtrodden, scummy mummies, either. Mum has always been a looker even when she was pushing a pram and doing the big shop. Wherever she went, she garnered attention and it wasn't long before another man was wooing her.

When I was five, Mum met a new guy called John, who started off great. He was so friendly whenever Regan and me were around and we were pleased he was in our life. It was only after a few months of knowing each other that Mum and us moved in with him. And a couple of months after that she was pregnant again. You can imagine how fuming I was about that: it had taken me a good while to get used to having a little brother, but now my mum was having another child to add to her brood.

She didn't find the pregnancy easy, and neither did Regan and me, but after nine exhausting months, she finally gave birth to my sister Paris in November 1997. Both Mum and John completely doted on this new little girl. I felt kind of pushed out when she came along because Mum, John and Paris were one family unit, and because Regan and I had a different dad, we seemed like outsiders.

I know that feeling wasn't in my own head, either. I'm not just saying all this for effect; that's how we were made to feel, especially by John. Because Regan and I weren't his children, he didn't love us in the same way he loved his own child, if he ever loved us at all.

I don't want to unnecessarily slag the guy off because he is still my sister's father and all credit where it's due, he has been a very good father to her. I can't take that away from him, but I can only tell you about my impression of him and it's not a very good one.

My overriding feelings about John were that he was a mean person. I knew it from the way he would look at me, scold me and become frustrated by me. After all, I was only a six-year-old girl who should have been enjoying her childhood, but I was completely intimidated and frightened by this man.

Regan and me were treated so differently from Paris. Even though she was only a baby, Paris had a massive bedroom to herself, while my brother and I were made to share a bland box room, which had no decoration or anything. It was like the room where you stash all your junk when you can't be bothered to throw it out, with a bed for us to sleep in. Where I come from it's not unusual to share a bedroom with your brother or sister, though – many of the families struggled to cope without much money or opportunity knocking around.

Despite being so young I was still old enough to know when we weren't welcome. Most nights, we would be made to eat our food off plates on the stairs, while John, my mum and my sister Paris would be all eating at the table. It was being excluded like that which made us feel unwanted and it's a horrible feeling to have in your own home.

I know what you're probably all thinking: 'Why didn't you tell your Mum about the way you were feeling, Lateysha?' So let me make this clear… from the beginning my mum and me had quite a cold, frosty relationship. And it has been like that all the way through my life up until about two years ago. I don't think I ever had cuddles, or had her tell me she loved me in the way that most mums do. Our relationship now is much better, but growing up it was very emotionless. I couldn't really speak to my mum about some of the concerns I had about John because I didn't want to upset her even more. Like I told you before, she was suffering with depression. She didn't need me to heap any more grief on her.

Later, John became very abusive to my mother, Regan and me. On more than one occasion I would see him lash out at her, while she cowered against the wall. Other times, I would hear blood-curdling screams, which made me stop in my tracks and I would be forced to listen to him hitting her. Terrified, I would just cry and scream. I hated it when they argued, fearing for the whole house.

We were all frightened of John, especially when he flew into a rage. Unkind and dislikeable, he was also extremely controlling. He was an insecure person and wouldn't even let my mum go to the shops without him questioning exactly where she had been and what she had been doing.

There are so many things I could go into here, but what I remember most was the little things. Like when he would be putting us in the car and fastening our seatbelts, he would pinch our legs hard and tell us not to distract him driving. Or, whenever he walked past us, he would deliberately push us into a wall, making us lose our balance and fall down. Who does that to little kids? His behaviour was bullish, bizarre and nasty for the sake of it.

Of course my mum knew his behaviour was unacceptable but she felt trapped at the time. Also, John could be so nice at times and when he fucked up he would always apologise and say it would never happen again, although it always did. These days my mum stays very quiet on the subject. At the end of the day, he is still Paris's dad and she wouldn't want her to think badly of her father.

Another time, my little brother (who was still wearing nappies) took his nappy off and smeared the contents all over our bedroom wall. Obviously it was gross, but Regan was only young and he didn't know what he was doing. No one discovered what he'd done until the morning and by then you can imagine the smell. Instead of just relaxing and putting it down to kids' behaviour, John went completely berserk. He came into the bedroom, saw what Regan had done and became thoroughly enraged. Grabbing my brother by the arm, he swung him round to face the wall he had soiled. He kept screaming, over and over, 'Look what you've done, you dirty little shit!' My brother began to wail, but I was in a complete state of shock and just froze. I didn't know what to do – I wanted to leap in to defend my brother but I was terrified of what John would do to me too. He beat Regan and it was absolutely heartbreaking to see.

It seems so weird saying I watched John beat my brother, like it was something so matter of fact and regular. I now know that it's not, but when you don't know any different – how would you know that it's not normal to hit your kids?

At that time the whole household was perhaps unsurprisingly not a happy one. In fact, it was terrible. I was glad to go to school because I knew I would be safe there. All my friends used to hate school, but for me it came as a relief, providing an escape from John and his ugly moods. I would literally do anything to get out of that horrible, aggressive environment. I remember once some Jehovah's Witnesses came knocking on the door and tried to speak to my mother about their beliefs. She wasn't interested in what they had to say and told them to leave but I begged them to take me with them on their house calls. They didn't mind and my mother, after seeing how desperately I wanted to go, gave her permission. Of course most mothers wouldn't let their six-year-old girl go off with strangers, but I guess she needed the break from me, too.

So I spent all day with them, knocking on doors and listening to what they had to say about their religion. I wasn't concerned about any of it, I just needed to be away from John, that house and all the screaming that went on there. The couple who took me around were really kind and friendly to me. At the end of a couple of hours' door knocking they would return me back to my house and say I'd been as 'good as gold and could go again whenever I wanted'. I never really spoke to them about why I wanted to be out with them so much; I think they just thought I was some crazy, outgoing child.

Eventually, my mother and that low-life John split up because he'd been having an affair with another woman. He was constantly cheating on Mum throughout the whole relationship, which is probably why he always suspected it of her. There's a saying, 'the evil you see is the evil you do', and that's obviously why John was such a suspicious snake: he was tarring Mum with his own brush.

I was over the moon when it all ended, but my mother was

gutted. Don't get me wrong, these days, she looks back and is thankful they split, not only for the way he was treating her, but they way he was treating me and my brother. But back then she was devastated. She was financially dependent on him and we were living in his house. Obviously, still young, I didn't think about such repercussions; I just wanted him away from my family as soon as possible.

John let us stay in his house for a while until one day, a few months later, he decided he wanted to move back in. He said he'd given my mother enough time to find another place and she would have to be out by the end of the fortnight. Mum was frantic at that time: she had three kids and no idea where we were going to live. I remember her sobbing her heart out because she had no idea what would happen to us all and John was being so incredibly unreasonable.

We literally had nowhere to go. You would think John wouldn't want to kick a young woman out of a house with three children to see her living on the streets, wouldn't you? But that's exactly what happened. It didn't even matter to him that one of those kids was his own daughter.

Often I would hear Mum cry herself to sleep at night. She was sick with worry that we would end up on the streets. While I wished I had the answers, I didn't, and I felt anger towards John for doing this to our family.

Mum had been in touch with family and friends but no one could help us with our situation. Then she got in touch with the local council, but they had nowhere for us to go immediately either. In the end the only option was to move into a women's refuge until we could eventually find our feet.

Unless you've been through that situation, it's impossible to imagine how hard it is to leave your home and move into a new environment like a women's refuge. I have to say it's completely soul-destroying and my mum was so unhappy.

Mum tried her best to protect us from the shock of moving from a house to a communal space. She told us, 'Kids, we are going to have to move, but we all need to stick together. Look after each other and everything will work out for the best.' We would be living with other people and we were to be on best behaviour, she explained. To cushion the blow, she made out it would be like a hotel.

She felt like a failure, like she had let her children down. Of course, I was too young to understand all of this, but now I can't help but feel sorry for her. Mum has made some bad decisions in life, but nothing so bad that she deserved to be treated in the way she sometimes was. She couldn't unload her problems onto me, but luckily there were many women at the refuge who were sympathetic. They understood what she had been through and she found their support invaluable, at least that's what she tells me these days.

Going from a decent-sized house to one scummy room was a tough adjustment for all of us. In our room there was a double bed, a wardrobe, a sink and a camp bed that was covered in stains. The walls were completely blank and the carpet was threadbare. All the other areas of the refuge, like the kitchen, living room and bathrooms, were communal. I don't remember much from this time, probably because I'm embarrassed and try to block it out, but I do remember we would be starving but had to wait our turn until other women were done in the kitchen before my mum could feed us.

Mum was completely devastated. Often I would see the mist of tears forming in her eyes. No one ever imagines having to bring up a family in a refuge and she forever blamed herself for this whole situation. Mum didn't really speak about anything at the time, not with us kids anyway, but I would overhear her talking to others. 'I've got three kids, no house, no money, no security, nothing... what am I going to do?' she would cry. 'I never thought my life would end up like this. I can't believe what he has done to us.' It was upsetting to see Mum like that, because around us she would attempt to put on a brave face and tell us everything was going to be fine.

We had arrived at the refuge with very few possessions but luckily the staff provided the basics, like food, nappies and toiletries until my mum could secure welfare benefits, enabling us to live independently. And then a few weeks later we were moved on to a council house not far from my school.

It was a huge relief being out of the refuge, but I worried for Mum, not having all those other women to talk to. You see, once you have lived with domestic violence, you are never quite the same. Her self-esteem was very low and I knew it would be a long time before she would be able to rebuild herself. Having other people around her must surely have helped – it was like therapy in a way, I suppose.

As soon as John was out of the picture, life got better. To be honest, it couldn't have been much worse. But when it was just my mum, brother, sister and me, I loved it. I look back on those times fondly. There was no arguing anymore or fighting, we all got on together and had a really happy time. I wasn't desperate to leave the house at any given moment; I was content to play with my siblings, watch TV and make a mess without fear of being screamed at by John.

Despite my concerns, my mum was regaining her old self back, too. She was going out a lot more with her friends to the local pub. I suppose after being on her own with kids all the time and going through a break-up she needed some kind of release, which I can understand now. At the time I just felt like she didn't want to be with us and we were constantly being babysat by this person or that. To see her happy was great, though – it meant there was life after all the abuse. I know now that the psychological damage that happened couldn't be erased overnight, but at least our lives were being rebuilt, Mum was rediscovering herself and she began to enjoy what life had to offer. John stayed in touch with Mum, really only for the sake of Paris and, like I've said before, he is a good dad to her. They have a positive relationship and one that I wished I'd had with my father.

I was just so happy my mum was getting back to her old self. We were all getting along and, for now, life was good.

Chapter Three

FATHER FIGURE

It wasn't until I was about ten years old that I met my real father for the first time. Since I'd been born, I'd never had one phone call, a birthday card or even a Christmas present from the man. He never helped my mum financially, either, so for him to make the effort to come and see us was a big deal. When Mum told me he was coming to visit, I couldn't believe it; I was so deliriously happy. I'd always been interested in finding out what kind of guy he was and now I'd finally be able to put to rest some of my searching questions. Every time I'd seen any black guy walking down the street, I always wondered, was that my father?

He came one Saturday afternoon and when we finally met for the first time, I couldn't stop crying. Tears of joy, I might add. I was taken aback by how good-looking he was. About 5ft 11in, he was muscly, with his hair fashioned into twists. He looked like Craig David, with a mole on his lip.

He walked into the living room and said, 'Hello, Lateysha, I'm your dad.' It felt weird, this complete stranger saying he was my dad, but I was comfortable with him right from the get-go. I never once thought, this man hasn't been in my life for ten years – it was like we hit it off straight away. He was so cool and friendly, I remember thinking. At that moment, I was proud to call him my father. I looked up at his face and even though I think I look more like my mum, there was some slight resemblance between us. We had almost the same mannerisms despite never having met before. Regan was ecstatic. You know what little boys are like with their dads. He gave Dad a massive bear hug and a huge kiss on the cheek. It was really lovely to see and when you compared Regan to my dad, they were the image of each other.

We didn't have much planned, so Dad took it upon himself to think of something to do. He took my brother, my friend from our street and me out for the day, to a place called Margam Country Park, about half an hour's drive away from our house. A stunning beauty spot, it was the complete opposite of Port Talbot, which I rarely left. There was a kids' adventure play area, which we climbed all over, and then we spent hours walking around the huge gardens. There was a massive lake in the middle of the grounds; we walked round it and fed the ducks. I remember it being a great day out.

Dad's behaviour had been impeccable and when it came to him leaving, I was gutted. I remember crying when he got in the car to go back to Birmingham. I made him promise to come and see us again soon, a promise he swore to me he wouldn't break. He left with me feeling on a high because finally, I knew where I'd come from. Regan was happy too; even though he was really young at the time, we have spoken about it since and we both remember having such great memories of that day.

I had never even seen a picture of my dad before that day, so you can imagine how good it felt for me to see him for the first time in the flesh and put a face to a name. Most kids take the fact they have a dad around for granted, but imagine you'd never clapped eyes on 50 per cent of your genes until the age of ten. It was a momentous day and I'm glad, at least, our first meeting was filled with happy memories.

The next time I was due to see my dad was for Regan's sixth birthday, a few months later. Since our first meeting he had called a few times to see how we were getting on and always promised to come back to Wales and take us out. He was never specific about arrangements but I hoped whenever he was free, he would jump in the car and make the three-hour journey to our house.

On the eve of my brother's birthday, Mum called us both down from upstairs and told us she had a surprise for us. Regan and me stood there smiling as she said, 'Your father, Leroy, is going to come to your birthday party, Regan.'

'*Really*, Mum?' we both responded in unison.

'Yes, he will be here tomorrow afternoon, so I want you both to look extra-special.'

I was so happy, I could have burst – we hadn't seen him in months and I had hoped now we had met properly, these visits would become a regular occurrence.

The next day we both dressed up, just as Mum wanted. It's crazy how you remember some details and not others growing up, but that day I know exactly what I wore. I had on a pretty gingham dress, my mum put my hair in bunches and I had my favourite white lace frilly socks on too. Regan was looking equally smart in his button-down shirt, which I helped fasten up for him, and khaki green trousers. My mum had even made extra-special effort with her hair and make-up. She would never admit to that, but I could tell. And who can blame her? Every woman wants to look her best, especially in front of an ex. The house was immaculate, the weather was beautiful and we had balloons, games and a cake we could light with candles. Everything was set: it was going to be perfect.

Dad was due to arrive at 2pm, but it was already 3pm and there was still no sign of him. 'He must be stuck in traffic,' my mum said, making an excuse for the delay. 'There's probably been an accident on the motorway.' Any time we heard a car drive past the window, Regan and me would bolt from the couch to see if he was pulling up, but every time we were disappointed.

At 4.30pm he still hadn't arrived. By now I was beginning to get worried – I hoped he hadn't been in a car accident or something. I had this feeling in my tummy; I suppose it was disappointment, but I kept wishing he would soon be there.

It was actually 5.30pm before he rang to tell us where he was. I could only hear one side of the conversation but after a few words my mum took the phone in the kitchen and shut the door so we were out of earshot. I knew then this wasn't going to be good.

When she returned, she looked forlorn as she told us, 'Your father isn't coming.'

Heartbroken, I had been so excited and now my dreams were crushed.

'Why? Why doesn't he want to see us, Mum?' I pleaded.

'He does, Lateysha. He is very sorry, but he has been caught up in some... trouble,' she said, tailing off.

My dad had called my mum and told her he wouldn't be coming to his son's birthday party because, get this, he had been shot in the leg! I've heard some excuses in my time, but this has to be one of the most shocking, so shocking that it had to be true.

Now, I knew virtually nothing about my dad so I didn't know if he hung around in circles where being shot was the norm. I just knew when my mum told us, I was completely crestfallen. After that first meeting I had built my hopes up so much; I had been so excited to see him again. Now, not only was he not coming, I was scared he was going to die. The only times I'd seen people being shot was in the movies and they always died. I was crying uncontrollably. Mum tried to calm us down and explained that he'd been coming out of the barber's. He had been gunned down by another man and robbed of all his jewellery, but he was going to be OK. She said he was gutted that he couldn't be with us for the party and would make up for it when he was feeling better.

The whole scenario sounded outrageous and somewhat dodgy to say the least. It was only then that it occurred to me that my father was obviously a shady character. I didn't, for one second, buy into the fact that he had been innocently shot just as he was walking out of the barber's.

Deep down I knew, no matter how much I wished it to be different, this man was never going to be the dad I wanted. The kind I could call up for advice, rely on to help me with my maths homework, to vet my future boyfriends, give me pocket money, soothe me when I was upset, wipe the tears from my eyes, scowl when I was bad but praise me when I was good. We are supposed to be inspired to act like our fathers, not shudder at the thought. Still, I wished with every fibre of my being that at some point soon he would start taking an interest in me. Given the fact that he hadn't been bothered for the first ten years, this was perhaps a long shot but a girl can always live in hope.

Not long after the 'no show' from Dad, my mum took me to her best friend Suzy's house. I thought we were just going round so she could have a coffee and gossip as she usually did, but on arrival, I realised there had been an ulterior motive. I walked into the house and sitting there was this guy I didn't recognise: dark hair, piercing blue eyes and with a well-toned physique you could see through his shirt. As soon as he saw me, he rose from his chair and I was impressed by how tall he was. He was pushing 6ft 3in, but to me at the time he seemed much taller, like a giant.

He smiled a big toothy grin, which was so friendly it was disarming. It was like his eyes lit up when he saw me for the first time.

Crouching down so his tall frame was at my level, he softly said, 'Hello, you must be Lateysha. What a pretty name for a little girl! These are for you.' He handed me over a bag of Haribo Starmix. From the off, I was completely floored by this guy. I beamed back at him, amazed at his generosity.

'What do you say, Lateysha?' my mum said.

'Thank you so much!'

'This is Craig Ryan, Lateysha, my new boyfriend,' Mum explained, while Craig looked at me, still smiling as he waited for my reaction.

I beamed at the pair of them and in that moment, I was delighted my mum had finally found a new guy and one who seemed to be such a gentleman. All afternoon, Craig was attentive, sociable and interested in me. It was such a stark contrast to what I had been through with my mum's last partner, John. We played and watched TV for hours. He asked me endless questions about myself and he made me feel like the centre of attention.

By the time we left to go home, I was completely besotted. Giddy with excitement, I absolutely idolised him. He was so warm, welcoming and friendly. I'd been instantly won over by his strong, charismatic smile right from the first moment I met him.

'What did you think of Craig, Lateysha?' my mum asked.

'He is amazing, Mum! I really like him.'

'I think he is amazing, too,' she said, smiling.

I knew then by the look in her eye that she was serious about him.

Finally, this could be the father figure I've been looking for all my life, I thought.

Chapter Four

JEKYLL AND
HYDE

y mum's relationship with Craig moved on fast, as it did with all her relationships. It seems that when any guy got with Mum, he wanted to tie her down by committing to something serious very quickly. It's a testament to my mum herself because she is so easy to get on with – friendly, fun and gorgeous too.

I absolutely adored Craig. Like I said, from the moment I met him he made such a massive effort with me and I kind of felt after all the frogs my mum had been with, this was her prince. After I met Craig, my mum introduced him to Regan and Paris shortly after. They too thought he was a cool guy. It helped that I had already given him the seal of approval and they both generally followed what I thought because I was the eldest.

Craig held down a good job at a local steelworks. A contractor there, he earned a really decent wage and was well respected. He was twenty-six, young at heart and he treated my mum well. I had never seen her this happy in all my life. So happy, in fact, that after six months of being together, they decided to get married. Mum had been in a few serious relationships but she had never been married before, which to me spoke volumes: it meant she knew Craig was different.

I remember when they sat me down and told me, a huge smile spread across my face and my eyes lit up. This was my chance to have a proper family and a proper dad in my life, one who was going to be there for me, who wasn't abusive to my mum or my siblings. One who was going to look after us, protect us and be reliable.

I gave them both a genuine hug and it was clear to them they had my blessing.

They bought each other rings and were excited to be planning a small, low-key wedding, in which both our families would be brought together as one. Craig already had two kids by another woman and my mum was keen to involve them in the celebrations because she wanted this relationship to work for everyone, right from the very beginning.

I was to be bridesmaid, along with my little sister Paris and Craig's daughter Jasmine. Regan and Craig's son Joe were to act as ushers.

The theme for the wedding was gold and cream. Mum's dress was a beautiful ivory strapless classic and she'd picked a similar one for me to wear on the big day. It was a little cream dress, which stuck out with the help of a tutu and a gold empire line band around the centre. I loved that cute dress, I felt like a princess wearing it.

When the wedding day finally came around, in May 2002, I was ten and as much as I should have been happy, I wasn't. I don't know why, I just had this weird feeling about the union between my mum and Craig. At the time I put it down to nervous excitement, but something inside was irking me. Don't get me wrong, I thought the guy was amazing, but I just felt I should have been happier than I was.

The wedding ceremony was held in a registry office in Neath, Port Talbot, and the reception took place just down the road at a place called The Naval Club. All my mum's side of the family had come from Scunthorpe to attend the nuptials and it turned out to be your typical Port Talbot wedding, including the fights. Mum's family are quite rough and once they've got a few drinks inside them, they can get rather overexcited. I don't know what they ended up brawling over, but this was nothing out of the ordinary. And hey, it's not a proper Valleys wedding if there aren't a few bust-ups and tears!

Around this time my Aunt Donna, my mum's sister, was going out with a guy called Kevin. When I met Kevin, I instantly disliked him. He was a scruffy character, a complete no-hoper. It stunned me that my aunt would even bother with a man like that. Every time I met him he was always bladdered and swinging his limbs around, like he was off his face.

Mum, Craig, Donna and Kevin would hang out a lot – double date, if you will – and I hated it. I didn't like Kevin being round our house and I hated that my knight in shining armour, Craig, was getting close to him. Why anyone thought this man was all right truly astonishes me, even to this day. I never said anything to my mum about how I felt. I kind of thought it wasn't my place to say anything. These days I wish I'd been vocal, but then again would anything have changed?

But I couldn't worry about Kevin too much because my mum was now expecting another baby with Craig. Within six months of them being married, she was up the duff again.

I remember the day Mum told me she was pregnant. I cried my eyes out. Up until then I was so happy it just being me, Regan and Paris. I didn't want anyone else to be involved in our family and I couldn't understand why my mum wanted even more kids. Already she had three and Craig had his own two. She used to say, 'Wait until you're in love with a man, Lateysha, there's nothing more special than having a baby with that person.' I kind of got where she was coming from, but I hated change. The house was cramped enough as it was and I didn't want another screaming baby around the place.

Heartbreakingly, as soon as my mum became pregnant things started to go drastically downhill with Craig. At first it was just the odd few cross words, but as time went on these erupted into blazing rows. Craig would be at work most of the time and when he wasn't, he would be out with that scruff-bag Kevin, coming home pissed and looking completely dazed. My mum would notice but longed for the Craig that she'd met and fallen in love with to return.

Before they were married I rarely heard Mum and Craig arguing, but now it seemed like that's all they did. He used to blame it on her hormones from the pregnancy, which I can believe doesn't help matters, but he should also have been there for her instead of constantly going out and spending money on getting lashed up.

Within just a few months of them being officially wed, I began to wonder if they had rushed it. This was not the Craig I knew and loved; he had become like Jekyll and Hyde. One moment he was lovely, cuddling and kissing my mum, the next he was screaming and shouting at her. I really hoped that when the new baby arrived, Craig would completely fall in love again and once again be the great dad I knew he could be.

Chapter Five

DADDY CRUEL

I think because of all the rows between Craig and my mum, there was tension in the house and I must have felt like I needed to turn to someone else. That was my main motivation for getting in touch with my father again. I was twelve and despite him being absent in my life while I was growing up, I still wanted to build a relationship with him. The first time we met had been so great, I wanted to try and rekindle the affection. If anyone could listen to my woes involving my mum and stepdad, it would be my real dad, surely?

I asked my mum if she would help me or if she had any way of contacting him. At first she tried to put me off the whole idea. I suppose she didn't want me to be disappointed again, but I just saw this as being uncooperative.

'Please, Mum,' I said, 'just tell me how I can contact him.'

'Lateysha,' she would say, 'he's not a very nice man. He hasn't been there for you in twelve years, why would you want to get in touch with him now?'

'I want him to be in my life.'

'But he doesn't want to be in yours. If he did, he would be,' she explained.

I knew she was right, but hearing those words cut through me. My biological father hadn't ever wanted to know me, but still I persisted.

'Maybe you're wrong, Mum. Maybe if I make the effort with him, he will want to make more effort with me. I just want to try and speak to him.'

Regan felt the same as me. He always thought I knew best because I was his big sister, so when I said I wanted to contact Dad, he also wanted to get in touch.

Mum had no way of contacting him so I decided to look for him on Facebook. A search on Leroy Henry in the Birmingham area proved fruitless so I decided to look for his sister, my aunt. When I had met my dad, he talked to me about his family and I always remembered his sister's name because it was so unusual. She is called Shubourne and I found her pretty easily and sent her a message. I wrote:

Hi Shubourne, I'm sorry for contacting you in such an impersonal way, but I had no other way of getting touch. My name is Lateysha and I'm your brother Leroy's daughter. I don't know if you have any contact with him, but if you do, can you tell him I would like to get in touch. I've attached some photos of me and my brother Regan. I hope you can get back to this message. Many thanks, Lateysha X.

I sent her a photo of me at school; also one of my brother playing rugby. I don't know why, I thought it would be harder to say no to me if she could actually see a picture of me looking smart.

She replied to my message a day later. The reply was short and sweet, thanking me for sending the photos, and she commented that we both looked lovely. She didn't have a number for our father, but she gave me the number of his father, our granddad: Donald Henry.

When I called my grandfather, he was so happy.

'Hello, Lateysha,' he said in his thick Jamaican accent.

'Hi, Donald.'

'It's been years and we still haven't met, girl!' he laughed and then said, 'How old are you now? I need to meet you. How come you don't ever come down here?'

'I'm twelve. Ah, I dunno why I haven't been before...' I said. 'Hopefully we can see each other soon. I was wondering if you had the number for my father, Leroy? I want to contact him and meet up.'

After about five minutes of chit-chat, he passed on my dad's number, which I wrote down on a piece of paper for safe-keeping.

When I'd finished the conversation with Donald I stared down at the phone number for a while, twisting the paper in my fingers and feeling sick to the pit of my stomach. I had nervous butterflies flying round my tummy. Crossing my fingers, I closed my eyes and prayed when I phoned my father that he would be happy to hear from me.

It wasn't until about an hour later when I finally plucked up the courage to call him. I was standing outside in the front garden, out of Mum's earshot. I didn't want her to hear my conversation because she hadn't wanted me to call him in the first place. Regan wasn't with me at the time; I thought I'd gauge Leroy's reaction before I told him.

When I heard the phone ringing, my heart raced. I was so nervous, I had baited breath – scared of the rejection, I suppose.

'Hello?' a man's voice said.

'Hello, is that Leroy?' I asked

'Uh, huh.'

'Oh, hi, Dad, it's Lateysha,' I said excitedly.

I heard a sigh on the other end of the phone and instantly my heart sank.

'How did you get my number?' he asked.

'Um, I got it off… um… your father.'

'Where? Who? Who gave it you?' he asked again, slightly more annoyed this time.

I'm not going to lie, I was gutted; this wasn't the way the conversation was supposed to go. In my head, I had envisaged him being over the moon to hear from me. I hoped he'd shriek down the phone with glee, like the way those long-lost families on *Surprise Surprise* do, who see each other after all those years and are overcome with emotion.

'Your father, Donald,' I repeated, 'He gave it me.'

'Oh, OK. So, how have you been?' he eventually asked, awkwardly.

'Erm, I'm great…'

The conversation continued like this for a short time. Stilted, just asking the small pleasantries, like any two strangers would.

'So, Dad, I was thinking of coming to visit you. I'll bring Regan too.'

'Oh, really? That would be nice. When were you thinking?'

'I'm not sure, I'll have to ask Mum.'

'OK, but how will you get here? I have no money, Lateysha. I can't give you any money for your travel.'

In all honesty, I hadn't thought of how I would get there. I hadn't really thought past this initial phone call.

'It's OK, I will ask Mum for money.'

'You do that and then let me know,' he said, trying to get me off the phone. 'I'll speak to you soon. Bye.'

'Bye, Dad,' I said, as he hung up.

And that was that. The whole conversation had been an utter disappointment. I thought he might have been pleased to hear from me, or at least pleased at the prospect of seeing me, but I felt like it was a chore for him to even be on the phone. Still, I gave him the benefit of the doubt. He must have been shocked to get a call out of the blue from his daughter. Maybe it was unfair to expect a huge warm reception – he probably didn't know how to react.

My mum hit the roof when I asked to take Regan with me to see him. He was only nine and she didn't want him being around my father because she used to say he was a nasty man. I would hit back at her with accusations about Craig being nasty these days. And so I begged and begged her until she eventually caved in. She also wasn't happy when she knew she had to pay for the trip, but she did give me the money because she knew how much it meant to me. At this time, my mum was working in a Chinese takeaway nearly every night just so we could make ends meet. She wasn't on very much money so she could only afford to send us on the coach (which took five and a half hours), but it was a whole lot cheaper than the train.

I'd planned my outfit meticulously a week in advance. I was wearing some cool jeans, a bright pink tee, a bomber jacket I hardly ever took off and a pair of Kickers. The whole journey there, I kept thinking about meeting him again. I kept playing out the scene where I'd see my dad, he would scoop me up in his arms and say he'd missed me – at least I hoped that would be his reaction, anyway.

Me and Regan were both so excited. We kept talking about

how cool our dad was and we wondered what kind of house he had, what he had planned for us. We literally couldn't wait to see him. I know you're probably thinking, why would you be excited to see a man who has done nothing for you for twelve years? Which is true: he hadn't been there for Regan and me when we were growing up. Because he wasn't there, he couldn't really hurt us, though. Not like my mum's first boyfriend John or my stepdad Craig, who was beginning to turn vicious with his angry mood swings, all the arguments and disrespecting of my mum.

Nervous anticipation coursed through my body as we arrived at the bus station. Seeing my dad again, I was overcome with emotion. I started crying with happiness. When I looked over at Regan, he too was so overwhelmed. The look on his face was amazing! I felt relieved to be finally reunited with my dad and just as I'd hoped, he scooped me into his arms and said he missed me.

In the car on the way to his house, Dad was pointing out bits of the city that were of interest as if we were on a sightseeing tour. As we neared the house he also said he had a surprise for us and I was excited to find out what it was.

I couldn't tell you what part of Birmingham we were in, but it didn't look the best. The houses were small and cramped, but I didn't care. I knew my dad wasn't an affluent man (none of my family were), but it didn't matter to me. I was spending four days with him and to me that was priceless.

Pulling up outside a terrace house, Dad got out of the car and grabbed our bags. As we walked up the small path to the door, an Indian lady opened it. Her name was Farrah and she was my father's new partner. Then we saw our surprise: it was his half-black, half-Indian son, Sky. Our half-brother was just a baby and an absolute cutie.

Before we left Port Talbot my mother had instructed us to be on our best behaviour and so I shook Farrah's hand quite formally and said 'Hello' as warmly as possible. My brother was quite shy, but he followed my lead and beamed a bright 'Hello' to this strange woman and her son.

Farrah was, in anyone's book, a beauty. She had the glossiest black hair down to her waist, thick, perfectly arched and plucked eyebrows, a big full pout and sparkling exotic eyes. I remember thinking, *What the hell is she doing with Leroy? She could have demanded millions to star in a Bollywood movie.*

Tell you the truth, her demeanour and beauty made me feel on edge. Even though I had been overly friendly, she wasn't. She was cold and distant at a time when I already felt out of my comfort zone. I know if it had been me meeting my partner's young children for the first time, I would have greeted them with open arms to make sure they felt comfortable, but as soon as we walked into the house, I got the feeling we weren't welcome.

I hoped and I prayed we hadn't made a huge mistake in going there.

Chapter Six

SHATTERED DREAMS

The first night at my dad's house went without any hassle. We sat around, chatted, laughed, watched TV, played with little Sky and ate one of Farrah's homemade curries before going upstairs to bed. My brother and I were sharing a small single bed, which was quite cramped but it didn't matter. I was content to be finally in Dad's house and as things stood, it looked like he would now be a part of our lives for good.

It was the next day that all the trouble started.

I woke up that morning with a loud yawn. I'd had hardly any sleep because Regan had taken up so much room in the bed. My eyes were half glued together when Farrah popped her head round the door to wake us up. It was still early and all I wanted was a few more hours, but I didn't want to laze about in someone else's house, either.

I started hunting through my bag for an outfit and laid out the clothes I was going to wear for the day on the bed: a little jumper and a short miniskirt. There were cute socks and some pumps to wear on my feet, too.

Seeing that no one was using the bathroom, I grabbed my toothbrush and went to brush my teeth. No sooner had I spat out the last bits of foam than I heard a shriek from the bedroom.

Pacing back down the hall, I asked, 'What's the matter?'

'Is this what you are wearing today, Lateysha?' Farrah asked with audible shock, pointing to my neatly laid clothes.

'Yeah, do you like it?' I said brightly, although judging by the thunder in her face, something told me she didn't.

Farrah didn't reply. She just walked out of the room, alarmed. I didn't know what I'd said or done, but I could tell it wasn't going to be good.

Moments later, she returned with my dad behind her.

'Have you seen what she's thinking of wearing, Leroy?' she shrieked.

I didn't know what to say or do. Dad looked at the clothes and he didn't say anything either.

'She cannot wear this! Lateysha, where is your bag?' Farrah roared.

'It's over there,' I said, pointing to my pink duffle bag, still in complete confusion.

Farrah grabbed my bag and pulled out all the clothes my mum had neatly packed for me. At the time all of them were pretty much the same – little skirts or dresses. Nothing outrageous, just cute clothes any twelve-year-old would wear.

'Look at this, Leroy!' she screamed as she held up a white short, pleated kilt, '*and* this!' as she grabbed my denim tutu.

I didn't know where to look. What was wrong with my clothes and why was she screaming about them? What was going on?

Farrah took all the items she deemed unsuitable for me to wear and went downstairs to the kitchen.

'Dad, what's going on? What's wrong with my clothes?' I asked, as tears welled in my eyes.

I ran downstairs after her, into the kitchen and to my horror, saw her cutting them all to shreds.

'What are you doing?' I screamed.

'Lateysha, these clothes are not suitable for a girl of your age. They are trampy and cheap! You can probably see everything in these skirts! How does your mother let you wear them?'

'Stop, I like them! Please stop!' I wailed. I couldn't believe what was happening and why my dad wasn't jumping in to stop her. 'I will have no clothes now. Please just stop, Farrah!'

'No, they are disgusting,' the mental bitch told me.

'Dad, please tell her to stop!'

By this time my dad was downstairs in the kitchen.

'Don't worry,' he said, 'We will get you new clothes.'

Heartbroken, I felt dirty and trampy now because of the clothes I'd brought with me. It was as if I wasn't good enough. Farrah took the pile of shredded material in her arms and out the back door. I watched as she lifted the lid to a metal bin, threw them in and lit a match. It wasn't good enough that she had completely shredded all my clothes, now she had to burn them too just to make sure they were completely destroyed.

At the time I was so upset, I couldn't stop crying. What an awful thing to do to a young girl! I get that in Farrah's religion young girls should cover up, but that's not *my* religion and I didn't want it forced on me. Such a distressing moment, it angers me so much to think about it now. Regan, bless him, put his arm around me when I was crying. I remember him having a five-pound note on him that my mum had given him and he said, 'I'll get you new clothes, Teesha.' He was so sweet.

As promised, they did buy me some new clothes but they were all trousers or long skirts, nothing like the ones I wanted. Heaven forbid that I would show my legs off! But that was just the start of the most horrible few days with Leroy and Farrah.

Neither of them had planned anything fun for us to do, so to keep us occupied, we were made to go upstairs and write out all the words in the dictionary. Can you imagine telling two kids to sit there and write out words from the dictionary, word for word? I kept thinking, *What the hell, this is supposed to be a holiday*! We just wanted to play, to go out and do something fun, but Leroy and Farrah were determined to make us do school work. It was like a punishment.

We did as we were asked for about an hour, but after that my brother had given up on writing his words and instead started doodling. Leroy came into the room and saw his pictures. Instead of laughing and perhaps complementing him, he screamed at Regan.

'What is this?' he said, ripping the paper out from under him. 'You making pictures when you should be writing!'

'I was just drawing, Dad,' he said, sheepishly.

'This isn't what we told you to do, was it, boy?' he shouted.

'I don't want to do that, Dad. It's boring! I just want to play,' Regan explained.

'Get back to your writing, Regan. Don't upset Farrah!' Leroy screamed.

'No, it's boring,' said Regan. 'I want to do something fun, I'm not doing what she tells me.'

'You will do those words, Regan, right now!' Leroy shouted.

'No, I am not,' my brother laughed. 'I am going to draw pictures. Ha, ha!'

'You laughing at me? No one laughs at me in my house!' I could tell Leroy was getting annoyed and agitated. 'You are going to learn to respect me and my wishes in my house!' he roared.

And with that, my father pulled back the leather of his belt to loosen the fastening. In a flash he whipped a fraying black belt out from his jean loops and fastened the buckle tightly round his hand.

In complete shock, I just froze because it was all happening so quickly.

He then proceeded to lash Regan with the belt on his hand. Five times he hit my brother. Every time his face contorted with increasing anger. I'll never forget the sound of the leather thrashing against his palm or my brother's horrific cries. Just thinking about it now, I feel sick to the stomach. We hadn't done anything wrong; Regan hadn't done anything to deserve being belted.

Almost instantly, I felt guilty. My mum had warned us not to go there and yet I thought I knew better. My brother had been so happy too. I cherish Regan more than anyone else in the world; I treat him almost like a son because he is my only full brother and to see this happen to him was truly heartbreaking. I thought Dad was going to welcome us with open arms and be the father figure we so badly craved. But no, he was just as abusive as all the other men so far in our lives.

I stepped in the way of my dad and Regan. If that cruel bully wanted to carry on belting him, he would have to go through me first. As I cradled Regan under my body, I left my back exposed to my father instead.

'Stop hitting him!' I screamed. 'He's done nothing wrong. Hit me instead.'

Eventually, Dad left the room as I attempted to calm my brother down.

'Regan, shhhhhh! It's OK, I've got you,' I soothed. But nothing I did was going to heal his bruises and I felt responsible for bringing him there.

The next day we went back home to Wales a day early and for us it couldn't have come soon enough. Farrah was made up when we were leaving too, so she could get back to her perfect little life with Leroy and Sky. My dad apologised to my brother and put his outburst down to a bad day. At that point I didn't care what he had to say, I just wanted him as far away from us as possible.

On the way home Regan and I decided we should keep what had happened to ourselves for a while. I didn't want my mum to be angry at me because of what had happened. I felt like it was all my fault. If I hadn't begged for her to let us go, Regan would never have been brutalised like that.

Back home, Mum met us off the bus and I've never been so happy to see her in all my life. We ran over to her and hugged her tightly. I wanted to cling to her and those precious few moments before we had to go back home and listen to more rows with Craig. Holding her, I just burst into tears and then I was truly sobbing.

'Lateysha, what's the matter? What's happened?' she gasped.

I was crying so hard, I could barely speak. Regan began to get upset too and instantly she knew it wasn't because we had missed her.

'Mum,' I wailed, 'we had the most awful time at his house! Farrah burnt all my clothes...'

'She did *what*?'

Regan was sobbing too and I thought he was going to tell her about what had happened to him. I looked at him straight in the eye and he knew instinctively by my facial expression that he must not say a word.

We put his weeping down to missing home and it was only years later we actually told her what really occurred. When she found out, she hit the roof. She was fuming we hadn't told her at the time. When she heard the full story she immediately banned us from ever seeing him. As far as she was concerned we would never meet our dad again.

These days Regan and me can't quite believe he did that. It's truly astonishing when we think back to it now. We both spoke about the incident not too long ago and we both agree it was completely out of order. I don't think we realised how traumatising it was at the time, but it really did affect us. In a way, we have to thank him, because if we ever have children we will never treat them the way he did. He showed us what it was to not be a father.

At the bus station, my mum didn't know what to do. She simply gazed at her two children, who just days ago she had excitedly waved off from the same spot in the bus station, who were now weeping, unbeknown to her, because of their brutal father.

She began crying, too. And the three of us just held each other tightly and wept.

Chapter Seven

LIVING WITH
THE DEVIL

As it turns out, I didn't know Craig very well at all and now, I was afraid to know who he actually was. Maybe I loved him because I didn't know. If I'd known what he was really like and where he was going in life, no one would have cared about him and that would have been the end of my mum's relationship. He could have been a flash in the pan, someone we never saw again. But now they were married and were having a child together, it wasn't that easy.

Towards the end of Mum's pregnancy, Craig had become unbearable to live with. He was slacking at work and his whole persona changed. Now he was spending more and more time with Kevin, going to late-night parties and not showing up for work. It was a complete switch from the man I'd first met.

Then the rumours began. When I overheard a few friends and family saying Craig had been using drugs, I was stunned. I was also upset and scared, but most of all, confused. How could I not have known that someone I loved was doing drugs? I'd grown up around some down-and-out druggies in Port Talbot; all my life I'd seen them in alleyways shooting up smack so I knew one when I saw one, enough to spot one living in my home, anyway. Deep down, I knew Craig was a junkie. It wasn't just something commonly used and deemed to be glamorous like cocaine either; Craig was using heroin.

I didn't want to believe it. To me, he was a decent man, with a good job and not some down-and-out scruff, using drugs and drinking himself to oblivion. He was married to my mother; there was a baby on the way, step-kids to look after... He didn't want to use drugs, did he? Wasn't he happy enough already?

Heroin use, like most drug abuse, is a highly secretive affair. Often, those closest to an addict have no idea the person is using and my mum completely refused to believe it. But after the rumours began, I started looking at Craig in a different light. His appearance changed – he began to get thinner, his face seemed to age into that of a wrinkled old man; his cheekbones were prominent and his face was hollowing. His youth was disappearing right in front of our eyes and there was nothing anyone could do about it.

I dismissed it at first and put the ageing down to the stress of his job, because often in the early days he would come home looking haggard. But we found out later that's where it all began – at his work – for he was taking drugs while on the site.

These weren't rumours anymore: he was not only using, he was addicted to heroin. I don't know why he started, but for some I suppose there comes a time when all the beauty in the world just isn't enough and they start chasing something else, an escape from reality.

The rows had been bad before, but when my mum gave birth to my brother Kason in November 2004, their relationship became marginally better. I'd say for about four months Craig tried to get on with everyone. He and Mum would sometimes share a joke and when he was happy, the whole house was happy. He'd got used to the idea of a new baby son in his life and adjusted well for a time. But just as everything was beginning to get better, something was round the corner, ready to fuck everything up again.

Unbelievably, after only a few months of Kason being born, my mum fell pregnant again. This pregnancy hadn't been planned, but she thought that because she and Craig had made some headway in recent months, he would be happy to have another child.

I couldn't believe it when she told me; I wasn't glad about it at all. What on earth was she thinking, having another baby? Already she had four kids and now she was expecting a fifth, with that bag-head Craig! You would think I might be used to this by now, wouldn't you? But no, it didn't get any better. Another bombshell was dropped on me and my siblings. It always hit me the hardest, probably because I was the eldest and was more aware of what was going on. When they told me I couldn't say or do anything except shake my head.

Don't get me wrong, when Kason arrived, I absolutely adored him. In fact, I loved him so much and because I was older now, thirteen, I looked after him all the time. In some ways, it felt like he was my baby. Mum was pleased because she desperately needed the help. But when she told Craig she was expecting again, he was livid. He should have been over the moon but he was anything but, and I honestly think that's what set him off on a downward spiral. Gone was the decent fella, who was trying to keep it all together for his new son. Soon we were back to living with the Devil who put the fear of God into my siblings and me.

The rows erupted again. I would hear the most horrific screaming and shouting, but because I was the eldest it would be my job to shield the other kids and keep them calm. Half the time, the arguments weren't over anything substantial, but because of the drugs you could see Craig and his behaviour rapidly changing.

He became paranoid, anxious and angry. Some days he would just sit on the couch, drowsy, his eyes sunk into the back of his head and completely out of it. Other times he would pace up and down the living room, swallowing because he had such a dry mouth and scratching his skin until it was red raw. His fingers were blistered and they smelt like lighter fluid, like burnt tin foil and rusted silverware.

He was a skeleton. His weight had plummeted and his clothes hung from his body. You could see his ribcage and the sight of him made me feel sick. Even though I didn't know much about drugs, it didn't take a genius to work out that Craig was now addicted, despite whatever he told us.

When Craig was in a bad mood, the whole house would be petrified of him. As children we all became introverted and dared not speak in case we upset him. It was such an awful time, and a dreadful feeling, to be treading on eggshells in our own home. He had become one of those men who sit in the living room, simmering. We always felt it, that fear – the sense that his unpredictability might, at any moment, cause him to break loose and do something terrible.

I remember a time when Craig chased Mum and me up the stairs. We had been downstairs in the kitchen, while all the other kids were sleeping. I can't really remember what set him off but he was angry about the way my mum had spoken back to him. He was in one of his tempers and we just wanted to escape. It was like in the horror movies, when the girl is trying to outrun the killer to get away from him and you groan because she flees upstairs instead of out the front door. But at the time it's impossible to think logically and we had nowhere else to run to. That day, my mum did all she could to appease him and luckily he calmed down before there was any physical violence. But there were other times when she wasn't so lucky.

And by 2005, when my sister Madison was born, everything good Craig had had going on in his life when we first met him had disappeared. He had lost his job, his looks, his humour; also, his ambition, his friendliness. His other children had virtually no contact with him and we all hated him. And my mum was deeply unhappy, but saw no way out of this horrendous relationship.

Craig's addiction was ruining his life and it became his number one priority to feed it, even before he fed himself. Heroin was his life now. Like, for example, when he went to the hospital to see my mum after she had just given birth. One of his relatives stopped him on the ward because she worked there, and after he mentioned he had been made a father again, she gave him a £20 note to buy a gift for baby Madison. So, did Mum ever see that money? No, of course not, but the local dealer did, when Craig left the hospital without even seeing Mum or the baby, and spent it all on heroin. Any money he would see would be handed over for a bit of brown within a matter of hours.

Another time he flew into a rage about something not being right in the kitchen (I think a few plates had been left out and he was going mental about it). At that time, Paris, Madison and me shared a bedroom. Paris had the top bunk, I had the bottom and Madison was in her cot. Craig's screaming had woken us all up and Madison, who was a few months old at the time, began crying at the top of her lungs. Mum came into our room to comfort her and shouted down to Craig to stop shouting because he was disturbing the baby, but this only made him more enraged. He ran upstairs, pounded through into our room and head-butted my mother straight in the face. I couldn't believe it. Terrified, I was powerless to stop it. What was I supposed to do in that situation?

Completely stunned, Mum began weeping. He tried to drag her up by the hair and told her to 'Shut the fuck up!' and get back into bed with him. Of course this is something no kid should ever see, but in our house it was the norm. Mum was petrified, there was nothing she could do but go along with what Craig said, so she told us all to be quiet and slowly slipped out of the bedroom.

To be honest, I don't know how she coped. I couldn't understand why she stayed with a man who was so abusive, so violent and so horrible to her children. I now know that his attitude had worn her down. Anyone who has ever suffered abuse will understand. She wasn't in control of her own life; it's not like she had a choice to leave him, and that's what most people find the hardest to understand. They say 'Why didn't she just walk out?' but you are mistaking her for someone who had a choice. Don't you think if she could have, she would have?

The house was in chaos and it was a horrible environment to grow up in.

Craig was pure evil. He was angry all the time, but if we dared be angry with him in return he would jump right down our throats. It was as if we were wearing strait jackets – but where else could we go?

At the time I begged Mum to leave him, but she would always ignore me and shout, 'Not now, Lateysha!' And like I said, I suppose if she had the option to escape she would have done so but things just weren't that easy. He was so controlling and manipulative too. Craig cut her off from all her friends and family so she had no one to turn to. If she had left him, he would have found her and either begged her to come back or done something terrible to her. She was too scared of him, so she just had to put up with his shit.

And believe me when I say there was a lot of shit. My mum never had much money from working in the Chinese takeaway but what little she had, Craig would steal from her. You could never leave anything around the house because he would take it all. He even stole the money she used to keep a roof over our heads to pay for his filthy habit.

We were so poor, we paid for our TV on a meter: it was a box attached to the back of the set and you would put money in it when you wanted to watch it. A man would come round every two weeks to empty it. It would be about 20p for six hours' worth of viewing. One afternoon, when Craig was desperate for money, he managed to pull the box off the back of the TV. He used a kitchen knife to prise it open and stole all the change out of it; there can't have been more than three quid in there. It wasn't only money that couldn't be left around, but all our possessions too. He would steal everything in sight and sell it on.

Although I never had much when I was younger, I remember three perfumes were given to me as a present at Christmas. I didn't realise at the time that Craig and his smackhead pal Kevin had stolen them from Superdrug in the town centre. Still, what I didn't know didn't hurt me and I absolutely loved them. One of my friends came round after school and I was so excited to show her and let her smell my new perfumes. When I went into my bedroom, I looked on top of the drawers where I kept them and they were gone. I searched high and low for them, even accusing my sister Paris of moving them, but she hadn't touched them. It was Craig: he had stolen them back from me and sold them on. I didn't know this for sure, but come on, who else would have done it? And when I challenged him he didn't deny it.

Another time I left my phone in the kitchen while I went upstairs to get something. I couldn't have been gone any longer than five minutes, but by the time I came downstairs the phone was gone and so too was Craig. After looking all over the house for it, somehow I knew, heartbreakingly, that my own stepdad had stolen it.

He also stole my brother Regan's PlayStation and all his games. My brother loved his PlayStation and it broke my heart to see him so upset because Craig had sold it. Mum had saved up for ages to buy it and I knew she wouldn't be able to afford another one any time soon.

But that wasn't the end of Craig's thieving. About a week later an elderly lady on our road was mugged. Two men ripped her handbag from her frail arm while she was walking to the shops. The shock of the event knocked her to the floor and she suffered some horrific bruising. It wasn't long before the police came to our house and arrested Craig (I think around £30 was stolen). Almost instinctively, I knew Craig was involved but the police could never prove it. I couldn't believe the depths to which he would sink just to feed his habit.

On another occasion, his mum had bought a new TV from Tesco. Craig went round to hers, took the receipt and went back to the Neath Abbey store, where she'd bought it. He grabbed the same TV as the one his mum had bought from the shelf, removed the security tag and took it back to the customer services desk to claim a refund. When I heard that, I couldn't believe how brazen he was. He never made off with the cash, though – the staff were already wise to his tricks, challenged him and he made a run for it.

Of course he ought to have been happy to get away with it the first time, but can you believe he actually went back to the same store to try the same scam? The police soon caught up with him and they pinned another theft on him in court, too. This time he had robbed gearbox oil and an engine fault code reader from Halfords.

To look at him made me feel sick. He was a walking bag of bones. His beaming smile and those pearly white teeth I'd loved in the beginning had become brown and it looked as though his body was rotting from the inside. I just hated living with him; our home environment was so abusive and upsetting, a distressing and dreadful place to be. I never wanted to be there, so I would stay out at my friends' houses for as long as possible until it was eventually time for me to leave.

After walking home I would go in through the back door. There was an alleyway behind the house and from there I could see our living room window. One night I came home and I could see Craig and one of his mates doing heroin in the living room. You couldn't miss the smell, either – it was revolting. Heroin has a very distinctive smell, a toxic odour, like plastic, fish and urine burning.

I entered the house and went straight upstairs to tell my mum. My siblings were all in bed asleep, but Mum was still awake. She went downstairs to check on what Craig was doing, but when she accused him of doing heroin, he just hit the roof. He began screaming in her face and then started screaming at me, calling me a liar. I stood there and took all his accusations. I didn't want to backchat anymore because I feared what he might do to me. Somehow he convinced Mum he'd just been smoking a joint and for some reason, she believed him. His dirty pal Kevin also backed him up. He kept saying to my mum: 'Chill out, we're only having some green, what's the fucking problem?' As if that was absolutely fine – to be smoking that around children.

Obviously she didn't want to cause any more conflict, she was just too scared of him.

He wasn't fooling me, though: it was quite clear what he was doing. Mum used to buy foil for cooking and in the end she had to stop because he was using it all. Being the eldest, many of the household chores fell to me, although we all pitched in a little. Sometimes when I would wash Craig's clothes I'd discover foil in the pockets. I would also find foil stuffed down the side of the toilet.

The only other person who knew for sure what Craig was doing was my little brother Regan. Craig would take him out onto the streets when he bought it and sometimes take him back to places – other people's houses – while he smoked it. Can you believe it? He took a child with him to some crack den while he got high. Regan was only eight years old at the time. Craig would threaten him with a beating if he told my mum what he was doing and Regan was too terrified to say anything to her, but he would tell me. Another time, when Craig was looking after Regan, three of his mates came to pick them both up and they drove to a rough council estate to score some drugs. They closed all the windows of the car and started smoking that shit with my little brother in there. Fucking hell, it makes me so angry. My brother and I only spoke about his recently and the whole situation boils my blood. My brother, now a big, strong eighteen-year-old rugby player, has often said he would love nothing more than to beat the shit out of him for what he did. But what's the point? Regan and I agree: he's not worth it. We wish nothing more than a slow painful death for him.

Even back then I hated Craig more than I've ever hated anyone in my life. There was so much rage inside me about the whole situation, I didn't know how to deal with anything. It got to the point where I just wanted to kill the man. I would daydream about ending his life by putting rat poison in his food or his coffee. I just wanted him out of our lives and the only way I could think to be finally rid of him was death.

Every night I prayed for something terrible to happen to him, which I know is not a good thing to admit to, but you must understand the trauma he put our family through. I didn't care that Kason and Madison wouldn't have a father because he wasn't being much of a parent to them anyway. All I could do was hope and pray for the worst.

I would find out later that I finally got my wish.

Chapter Eight

SCHOOL DAZE

Making the leap from primary to secondary school can be daunting for some youngsters, but not me. I couldn't wait to join big school; I figured it would be a new challenge, a chance for me to start over, meet some new people and mix with an older crowd. Two weeks before the start of term my mum took me to Primark to get my new school uniform. She didn't take me shopping very often, so it was a nice treat to be having a day out with her. Then she took me to the stationery shop, where I got all new pens, rulers, rubbers and a pencil case. I never really had anything new, and I vowed not to touch them until the first day of school; I wanted them to be pristine for as long as possible.

At the start of term at Sandfields Comprehensive in Port Talbot I met a girl called Cleo, who was in my class. We got on like a house on fire and fast became new best friends, forming a strong bond and spending nearly every second together. I would go over to her house all the time because as you all know by now, I hated being at home. Going to Cleo's was such a nice break, away from all the drama. Cleo's mum was a little crazy, though not in a bad way. In a really nice way, she was just barmy and really young at heart. She would always be dancing around, laughing and singing. It was like she wanted to be one of us, one of the girls. We didn't really look upon her as a mum. She would let us stay up late, ask us about boys, and I'm a little ashamed to say this but I wished my mum was like her. It's probably why I spent so much time with her family.

You see, no one in my school was flush with money but I still knew that I was one of the poorest kids. Everyone would come in on a Monday and talk about their amazing weekends, where both their mum and dad had taken them somewhere exciting. It got to me because I never left the house much and when I did, it would be to nip to the local shop. I never had a holiday abroad; I didn't have a dad I could talk to and do nice things with. Mum was becoming increasingly cold and distant from me and it broke my heart. I knew my life was very different to most: everyone had these seemingly perfect families, with a proper mum and a dad, and it served as a reminder that mine wasn't a nice complete family and never would be. To be able to dip into that lifestyle with visits to my friends' houses and doing things with their families made me feel included.

One of the best trips we ever went on was for Cleo's thirteenth birthday. Her mum hired a pink limousine, which drove us from her house to a kids' club night in Swansea. I remember thinking how lucky Cleo was because I would never get anything like that for my birthday. I had planned my outfit for the occasion meticulously. In my white vest, brown shrug, denim skirt and cowboy boots, I thought I looked absolutely stunning, like a member of Atomic Kitten or something. I felt really grown up and special in that limo and I loved the feeling – it made me feel important and I suppose that's why I've always craved the limelight and a VIP lifestyle.

When we got to the club, it was like no other place I'd been before in my life. I'd always seen people going clubbing on TV, but now I was finally in a grown-up club, I felt like I belonged. That night was one of the best nights I've ever had. I loved the loud music, the lights, the boys, the podiums, the dance floor; I was in my element. I climbed up on the platform and started shaking my ass to 'You Can Do It (Put Your back Into It)' by Ice Cube. Everyone gathered around me and started cheering. I'm not going to lie: I loved the attention and always have, even from such a young age.

After I got down from the podium, I remember this guy coming over to me and asking me to neck his friend. It seems so silly now that a guy would get his friend to ask me to kiss him, but I know everyone used to do it when they were youngsters, so don't even tell me you didn't! I looked over at the friend, who stood in the corner smiling at me, and the first thing I noticed was his massive braces. I hadn't kissed anyone before in my life and certainly no one with braces. I started panicking and asked my girls if I kissed him, would he rip my mouth open? They all assured me that Brace Boy wasn't a younger version of Hannibal Lecter and if I wanted to smooch him, I would be fine.

So, in true Lateysha-diva style, I flung my hair over my shoulders and strutted over to Metal Mouth. I didn't even say hello to him, I just grabbed him round the neck and started kissing him passionately. Despite his wired teeth, the lad was a great kisser and I absolutely loved the feeling of snogging a guy.

After that I got the clubbing bug and anytime there was an underage disco on, my friends and me would go. We would dance and laugh all night, but mainly we were there for the boys. We would literally snog anyone and anything with a cock between his legs, it didn't really matter what they looked like. As long as he had a mouth and a pulse we would pull him. At the end of the night we would count up how many guys we had scored with, like it was a competition to see who could be the biggest hussy.

It felt so nice to be wanted by a bunch of guys. I would be lying if I said I was desired by the lads in school, because I wasn't. In fact, I was bullied and teased by them on a daily basis. It was only little things, but with everything else that was going on at home it was so distressing at the time and I couldn't handle it.

My hair is Afro, obviously because I'm half black. To reduce the frizz, I used to wear it all slicked back and just have a bushy ponytail. But the boys would be cruel about my look. They would walk past my desk and start knocking on my gelled hair, calling me 'Concrete Head' and embarrassing me in front of the rest of the class. Then they'd say I had nits and greasy hair. It sounds so childish now to even think about it, but when I was young, I was so ashamed. The boys made me hate school to the point where I never wanted to go and as a result, my attendance suffered.

I would always 'mitch' from school ('mitch' basically means 'bunk off' where I'm from). I remember one time a girl called Rebecca and me were supposed to be in class but we skipped school and went to her house instead. Her parents were junkies and didn't care if we attended school or not, so we took our bikes and rode them to the nearest McDonald's.

We were sat laughing and eating our food when a lady who worked there came over to us.

'Hi guys,' she said, smiling broadly, 'so what school are you girls in?'

'Sandfields,' I replied, without thinking.

'And what year are you in?' she asked.

'Year 7,' I said, thinking she genuinely wanted to chat to me.

'OK, girls, clear up after yourselves when you've finished.' She said this sweetly and walked off.

I remember the next part vividly. After five minutes, just as I had a mouth full of double cheeseburger, I saw the headmistress and her 'mitching' man walk into the restaurant. Fear struck me; I didn't know what to do, whether to run, hide or come up with some crazy lie to explain why we were in there.

My mouth – still full of burger – just dropped open. The head stormed straight over to our table and yelled, 'Get back to school *now*! Get in my car immediately!' at the top of her voice. She caused the most horrendous scene, it was beyond embarrassing: the whole of McDonald's was looking at us.

It took me a little moment to register what was happening. I had to swallow my burger chunk without even chewing it, causing me to cough everywhere.

'I can't,' I said, still stifling coughs, 'I've got my bike, I can't leave it!'

'I can't believe I've had to come in here and see two of my pupils bunking off school! What have you got to say for yourselves?' she went on.

After a long pause we said, 'I'm sorry' in unison as Rebecca and me looked at each other.

'Right, the pair of you take your bikes home now and report back to me at school immediately after! Do not even try my patience any longer,' she screamed.

Rebecca went one way and I went the other, back to my house. When I got home I ran through the door, screaming for my mum.

'Mum, Mum!' I wailed, 'Mum, I've just had to run home from school.'

'*What*? Why, Lateysha, what's going on?' she said.

Between breaths, I managed to stagger out a sentence.

'Mum, it's horrible. I'm being bullied... by the boys... they are nasty to me,' I told her. By now I was beginning to weep.

'You're lying! What do you mean, they have bullied you?'

'They call me all kinds of names, Mum... they won't stop. I *hate* it there! I don't want to go back.'

'Right, I'm not having this,' she said, as she slipped on her shoes, 'I'm coming into school with you right now!'

The walk from my house to school only took us about ten minutes. All the way there, I told Mum what the boys had said to me about my hair and the way they tried to embarrass me. The more I told her, the more angry she became, until eventually when we arrived at the school gates I thought she was going to blow a fuse. I know I hadn't been quite upfront about the whole mitching from school thing, but still the rest was true.

She stormed straight into the headteacher's office and unloaded on her.

'My daughter has just had to flee the school premises because of the bullying and teasing. Why is no one doing anything about this? Look at her!' Mum pointed to my tear-stained face. 'She is distraught, I want these bullies punished.'

The headmistress looked completely bemused.

'Mrs Ryan,' she said, as she held out a hand to shake hands with Mum, 'let's just all calm down. Take a seat.'

My mother reluctantly shook her hand then sat down on the occasional chair in the corner.

'The reason Lateysha ran home today was because I have just found her playing truant in McDonald's,' the headmistress explained. 'One of the staff phoned me and told me two pupils were in there, so I made my way down and there they were: Lateysha and Rebecca, bold as brass, eating hamburgers.'

At this, my mother looked at me with real hatred in her eyes because I had lied and made a fool out of her.

'What? 'Teysha, is this true?'

What could I say? Now I couldn't lie so I played the only card I had left: I turned on the waterworks. I began to cry hard, so hard I could barely speak; I was struggling to catch my breath.

'Yeah, it is true,' I muttered.

Mum just tutted loudly and flared her nostrils. I knew she was absolutely livid with me.

'But the only reason I was mitching from school is because I'm being bullied,' I explained between sobs. 'The boys are so nasty to me. Every day they tease me and embarrass me in front of the whole class. I can't take it anymore!'

I began to tell my mum and the headmistress what had been going on during school hours. They both seemed to soften up after I told them everything. I didn't have to lie either, I *was* being picked on all the time. And it's not like I had any escape at home because Craig was the bully of the house. Recalling all this now, it's still so hard and it makes me wonder how I ever got through it all in the first place.

The head teacher vowed to step in and sort out the bullies, and to be fair to her, she did. My mum didn't step in and sort Craig out, but I understood it wasn't so easy as just giving him a telling-off. I didn't really get any grief off any of the boys again, which was a huge relief, but that wasn't the end of my problems at Sandfields.

Now it was like the bullying baton had been passed from the boys to the girls, and one girl in particular – the ringleader – was Samantha.

At one time we used to be friends, but I started seeing this guy Alex, who she fancied, which meant she instantly hated me. She was unbelievably nasty and turned everyone else against me.

Samantha was quite overweight and not pretty at all. What made it worse was my former best friend Cleo, the one with the cool mum, started to hang around with Samantha and after that I had no one. Cleo had been like a sister to me and now it was like I was a piece of dirt on her shoe. I honestly don't know why the sudden change and to this day I'll never understand.

Samantha and Cleo bullied me in some degrading ways. Leaving nasty notes on my desk. Purposely barging into me. Shouting insults, drawing horrible pictures of me and making snide remarks whenever I was around... until one day I just snapped.

We were outside Art and I had no way of getting to class without having to walk past the pair of them. I hurried along, darting past Cleo and Samantha, and making sure my eyes were firmly on the floor. I didn't want to give them any more ammunition to have a go; I just wanted to walk by in peace. That's when I heard one of them say, 'There she is, the frizzy head', while the other just laughed. But I'd had enough of all their behaviour. I literally saw red and screamed back at them.

'Who the *fuck* are you talking to?' I yelled.

'You, you're the only frizzy head around here!' Samantha sniggered. I'll always remember her big fat face as she laughed – I hated the way she laughed; it was so mean-spirited.

As I threw my bag off my shoulder, I knew I was about to explode. I pushed the fat, laughing cow straight into Cleo, knocking the pair of them over.

'Stop fucking laughing at me!' I shouted. I was so angry; I could feel my hand tighten into a fist. And that was it: as soon as I pushed them, all hell broke loose. We got into a huge fight outside the art building. All three of us were scratching, punching, kicking and pulling each other's hair. It was quite brutal, we didn't hold back. Eventually we stopped the fight and we all ran in different directions. It shouldn't have happened, but I couldn't deal with the way they were picking on me. I was in a complete daze about the whole thing.

Later that day I went home in tears to my mum. I told her all about the fight and how Samantha and Cleo were treating me. That night Samantha's mum came to our house to speak to my mother. She tried giving it all the fighting talk, but my mum explained how Samantha had been bullying me and obviously there's only so much a person can take before they eventually fight back; I had been pushed too far.

Now that I'm older, I've realised that Samantha must have hated herself for being overweight and butt ugly, because people who love themselves don't hurt other people. The more you hate yourself, the more you want others to suffer. There can be no reason other than that in my mind.

I begged my mum to let me leave Sandfields and to my surprise she did. A week later, I enrolled at St Joseph's Catholic Comprehensive and that's where I met my best friends: Casey, Harrison and Niamh. Meeting them was like a breath of fresh air and to this day, we are still unbelievably close. I loved every minute we spent together. Niamh became like a sister to me. She had the most gorgeous house and lovely parents; I used to love staying with her. Her family were so kind to me, they would let me go to church with them on Sundays and it was such a refreshing break from my own troubled family.

Even though I felt like I'd met my friends for life, I was still a very unhappy young girl. As soon as I went back to the horrible environment of home I would become depressed and feel worthless. It felt like I was living a double life, plastering on a smile at school and for my mates, and then when I was on my own I would be distraught. I didn't know how long I would be able to keep up the façade, or even if I wanted to anymore.

Chapter Nine

MIRACLE

If a miracle hadn't happened to save my life, I would have died at thirteen years of age.

I tried to committed suicide.

I know there are people out there who feel bad, and they feel like life sometimes doesn't make sense, but believe me when I say it's only temporary and you can get through it. Becoming a teenager is tough for any young girl. Your hormones are going wild, you begin to develop into a woman, your periods start and you have all these questions about love, life, sex and relationships. Then there's who you are and where you fit into everything, it's stressful. Most teens balance the bad with good friendships, success in school or outside activities and the development of a strong sense of self, but that never happened for me because all I could focus on was the horrendous stuff that was going on in my life at the time. All the shit Craig was putting our family through was just the most heartbreaking thing you could imagine. My home life was truly upsetting, shocking chaos.

Not only did I have to deal with all the usual teenage angst, I really was deeply depressed to the point where I just didn't want to be around anymore. I'm not just talking about bad moods and the occasional tantrum; I had a serious problem that was impacting on every aspect of my life. Depression was destroying the essence of my teenage personality and I felt an overwhelming sense of sadness, despair and anger.

At the time I didn't really know what was happening to me and I wasn't old enough to recognise the signs. Unlike an adult, who might have been able to seek assistance or counselling on his or her own, I couldn't. I suppose I was reliant on my mum or teachers to spot the warning signs, but Mum had her own stuff to deal with and by now, the teachers despaired of me.

It was like I didn't want to wake up in the mornings. I was having a much better time asleep and that's really sad. It was almost a reverse nightmare, like when you wake up from a nightmare you're so relieved; I woke up *into* that nightmare.

Not every day was as bad as the last. There used to be days when I thought I was OK, or at least that I was going to be. I'd be hanging out somewhere and everything would just fit right and I would think, *I will be OK if it can just be like this forever*, but of course nothing ever stays the same.

I don't think anyone really knew how bad things were for me; I never spoke to any of my friends about how I felt. And anyway, everyone had their own stuff going on. All the kids I knew in Port Talbot had pretty tough lives, it was a given. It's just some were worse than others.

Everyone coped with their stuff in different ways, but I took all these negative feelings out on myself. At this stage in my life I was self-destructing by drinking myself into a stupor to the point where I was paralytic. I would only have about £15, so whatever alcohol I bought was horrendously cheap. I would wait outside an off-licence and ask a likely adult to buy it for me. Vodka, cider or cheap wine, it didn't matter so long as it got me smashed. I would stand around in a field with a few of my mates and drink the whole lot as fast as I could. I didn't have any mixers or anything, I would just down it like it was water until eventually the pain and depression subsided.

When I was hammered from the alcohol I would feel so much better. It was the only time I could remember being happy. Of course I was self-medicating to get away from reality. In hindsight, I know what I was doing to myself was wrong. It was no way to live. I wasn't fixing the problem; I was blotting it out.

Every Saturday night was the same. Harrison, Casey and me would walk to a rough council estate called White City in Aberavon. The teenagers there were known as 'The Roughians' and you certainly wouldn't want to get on the wrong side of them. They were a dangerous gang, not the kind of people you would want your thirteen-year-old daughter to be knocking around with. I think, on some strange level, I hung around the worst places hoping to become injured or even killed – that's how much I didn't want to be around – yet all I could do was get drunk.

One night, I was looking forward to going out to White City with my friends. With a bottle of vodka and two small bottles of white wine stashed in my pockets, I couldn't wait to get off my face. But on the walk down there I had a huge argument with my friend Jade. I can't really remember what it was about, probably some boy we both liked. Jade was a stronger character than me and when we argued, I felt like I couldn't assert myself. She told me not to bother going to White City that night because if I did, I would be sorry. From the tone of her voice I knew she was serious and so I turned and walked in another direction.

I can't quite explain the upset. It felt like I'd been punched in the gut by one of my best friends. Abandoned and alone, I couldn't stop the tears from falling. My cheeks were soaked and all I could do was get away from the road so no one could see me crying.

Already the night was cold and dark, but I spotted a small alleyway in a place called Fairfield, not far from White City. It was behind a bank of shops and without another thought, I headed off in that direction. I didn't know what I was going there for, my mind was a complete blur of hopelessness, pain and anguish. My head felt fuzzy from all these horrendous thoughts and it was like I couldn't quite focus on any one thing; I felt dizzy.

I wandered down the alleyway until I reached a dead end at the bottom. The only brightness was coming from the orange street light above me. Huge, overflowing bins of rubbish stank but I didn't care, I was so sad my senses were numb to the smell.

I sat down with my back against the concrete wall, took out the bottle of vodka and gulped a huge shot of the bitter liquid, trying to warm up my body, which was by now freezing. As I sat there staring into the dark, my mind worked overtime and the tears came flooding. Over and over, I cried, focusing on all the bad things in my life at that time. I felt unloved. Unwanted. Useless. Stupid. Ugly. Pointless... I continued to drink until the last dregs of the bottle had gone.

After that everything grew hazy because of the vodka but my throat hurt because of the burning alcohol and I could sense the bile rising in my stomach. At that moment I could see no reason to keep going; I no longer had the courage to get past the pain. As far as I was concerned there was nothing good in my life to balance out the bad. I kept imagining everyone's life without me in it and I truly believed no one would care if I wasn't around anymore. I'm sure people would have been upset, but nothing they couldn't have dealt with. I felt like there was no one relying on me, even though my younger siblings were, and I didn't feel like I brought happiness to anyone around me.

I wiped the tears from my face and the snot and the vodka from around my mouth. In a complete state of delirium, I unscrewed one of the bottles of wine from my pocket and drained it in one gulp. Afterwards I almost heaved from the taste, which upset me even more. Self-destructing, I was in a desperate state and yet I had no one who cared – or at least that's how it felt to me at the time.

What was I doing in that stinking alley, drinking myself to oblivion, freezing, sobbing away and wanting to end my life? When I think back now, I can't help but feel choked up. At the time I felt completely abandoned and it still sends a shiver down my spine.

The second bottle of wine was still in my pocket and while it was there, I felt like I had something to live for: it needed to be drunk and I wasn't about to waste it. I unscrewed the cap, but this one was a lot more difficult. My fingers were so cold and I was so drunk, I could barely muster the strength to twist the lid off. Eventually, through deep sobs I managed to open the bottle and like the first, I consumed it in one enormous swig.

Now, I had nothing.

Nothing left to live for.

I felt sick and there was a searing pain in my stomach. Anything was better than feeling the way I felt that day, even death.

It must have been about two hours since I'd first walked down that alley. By now I was completely fucked from the alcohol and if anyone had found me in that state, they would have had my stomach pumped, for sure.

It's so hard to describe the deep despair I was in. Imagine

falling from a huge skyscraper and all you have to focus on is the sinking feeling in your stomach. You pray that the impact with the ground is quick because you need to end the sinking. That's kind of how I felt: I was sinking through life and it was killing me from the inside.

As I sat, I gazed around and tried to find the glass vodka bottle to maybe smash it and use the shards on myself, but it was so dark and I couldn't remember where I had thrown it. All I could find was a couple of bin liners next to me. My tears finally stopped and it was almost like I had some kind of clarity, a way out of my sadness.

I picked up one of the bin bags and without much more thought, tied it around my neck as tight as I could, so that it was cutting into my skin and slicing against my Adam's apple. I began to cough hard and my body started to heave from the alcohol and lack of air. It was hurting so badly, I thought my throat was being slit.

I was strangling myself to death. There's no other way to describe it. This wasn't a cry for help because there was no one around to see me do this; I actually wanted to end my life.

I staggered around, my face feeling hotter and redder as all the blood squeezed into my brain. Using one hand to steady myself against the wall, I continued to gasp for air. My heart began thumping uncontrollably when I knew there was a real possibility I might die. I could hear it beating louder and louder.

Then I saw it, the tiny miracle that saved my life.

I was hunched over, one arm leaning on the wall, the bin liner still wrapped tightly round my neck, the air escaping my lungs and my eyes focused on the floor. It took me a while to make out what it was (don't forget I was still blind drunk), but the adrenalin of the situation must have slightly sobered me up.

I saw a tiny ginger paw hanging out of the other bin liner on the ground. At first I couldn't be sure if I was hallucinating but then I could tell from the little pink pads and soft fur that they belonged to a kitten.

They say curiosity killed the cat but in that moment it was curiosity that kept me alive. Suddenly, my body's natural instinct for survival took over and I ripped the plastic bag from my neck. Once it was released, I took a huge intake of air and collapsed in a heap on the ground. It took me a while to get over the shock of what had just occurred. I was breathing heavily and my heart continued to thunder in my chest.

When I managed to regulate my breathing again, I peered down at the limp paw sticking out of the edge of the bin bag. Careful not to disturb it too much, I opened the bag fully and saw the little creature with its eyes tightly shut, just lying there – dead.

I'd never seen a dead animal before, not up close like this, anyway. Sure, I'd seen the odd squashed seagull in Port Talbot, but never something so innocent and beautiful as this kitten. I was in a complete state of shock. First, at what I had just done to myself and second, after the discovery of this small fur ball. I was instantly sad. Who could have done this to a defenceless creature? I looked closer and saw it had a piece of cable tied round its neck. It had been strangled to death and left to rot in an alleyway.

Half of you reading this won't believe me because it all seems too poetic and unrealistic, doesn't it? But I swear to you, as God is my witness, this actually happened the way I'm telling you it did.

I began to weep again and untied the cable from around the kitten's neck. I could imagine the pain the poor thing must have been through because I had just had a taster of it myself; the life being squeezed out of its lungs while it desperately cried and tried to fight back against whatever monster did this.

I wondered how long it had been left there. Maybe if I'd have noticed earlier, I could have kept the poor mite alive? But there was no way of knowing; it could have been there for days. I held the young cat in my hands and decided I couldn't just leave it there, so I moved to a patch of grass at the edge of the alleyway, dug up the earth with my bare hands and buried it.

I was still feeling the effects of the alcohol and some days I wonder if I imagined the whole thing because I was so smashed. But I know I didn't, because I still had dirt under my fingernails the next day from where I'd made a makeshift grave.

Other times when I'm on my own, I imagine what might have happened if I hadn't seen that kitten – would I even be here today? Would someone have found me in that alleyway, with a bin bag tied round my neck, limp and lifeless, too? It doesn't bear thinking about because now to look at me, I'm such a happy-go-lucky kinda girl but back then, when I was thirteen, life was completely unbearable. I never really believed in miracles and I don't know if what happened with the kitten could even be called a miracle, but who knows? I've always felt that someone or something put that little cat there as a sign and it saved me.

I never blamed anyone for what I did that day and I wasn't about to hold that argument against my friend Jade because we argued all the time about petty stuff. I was just going through a terrible time in my life and I couldn't think of a way out of it.

If I could give any advice to any teenager feeling the same way as I did, I would say, please don't think ending things is the only way out. Nothing is so bad that it can't be sorted or talked through; just find someone you trust and talk to them. You think you will end the pain if you take your own life, but that's not true, you will only be passing it on to those you leave behind.

Chapter Ten

HEROIN(E)

The episode with the kitten was a dreadful experience, quite possibly the worst I'd ever dealt with up until that point, but the most harrowing moment was yet to come. It happened when I had just turned fourteen, and I remember the grim reality like it was yesterday.

I was watching TV in the living room with my mum. My junkie stepdad Craig had volunteered to carry my little brother Kason (who was two at the time) to bed. He'd fallen asleep on the sofa while Mum was stroking his hair. At the time I thought it odd that Craig had offered to take him up – he usually forced my mother to do all the caring for us kids. I should have realised then that something was up, for his kindness in offering to carry Kason up to bed in his scrawny, needle-tracked arms was suspicious from the start.

A few minutes passed and my suspicions grew. I didn't trust Craig to have put Kason down properly, so I went up shortly afterwards just to check everything was all right.

The sound of my footsteps coming up the stairs didn't bother him – I guess Craig was oblivious to everything around him. As I approached my little brother's bedroom door, I halted. Seizing the handle, I leant towards it to try and work out if Craig was still in there. My fingers gripped the handle tighter and I leant my bodyweight into it, until the door slightly opened. I was half expecting Craig to shout at me for disturbing them but there was no noise.

The thick carpet stopped the door opening any further. It was a job Craig had said he would fix months ago. The door needed sanding down so it glided smoothly over the carpet, but as with everything else, he just never found the time.

With one hard push the door opened fully. My eyes darted about the room as if they were mad strobe lights. Nothing in the world could have prepared me for the shock of what I was about to see and the horrific scene will be forever etched on my memory.

I stood there, completely stunned.

Craig was collapsed on the floor in his dark blue pyjamas, a belt tied tightly round one bicep and a needle hanging out of his arm. The syringe was full of dirt, Craig's dirt. He wasn't moving and he didn't respond when I said his name.

'Craig, *Craig*!'

My eyes fixed on the hypodermic needle hanging from his arm. It was still half full with brown liquid.

Craig's body twitched, foam escaped from his mouth. Now there was vomit all over the floor and round his body; the room reeked of it. As I began to retch, I gazed at my stepdad in disgust. Through tearful eyes, I surveyed his convulsing body. I knew what was happening: he was dying.

He must have overdosed on heroin while my brother slept soundly. I was so dumbfounded that I just froze for a second before deciding what to do next. Right then, at that moment, I had a choice: I could raise the alarm, attempt to save Craig's life and ironically, enjoy heroine status for a time. Or I could close the door, walk away and do nothing.

If I shut the door, I knew Craig would surely die in the house in a matter of minutes.

For a second I thought about all the times I'd daydreamed about wanting him to die. Now that wish was finally coming true before my very eyes. In a sadistic way it made me want to smile and laugh; I wanted to let the bastard rot. For all the times he'd been abusive and mean to my family and me, this was finally payback. We would all be better off without him, no question about that.

I'd be lying if I said I didn't want to close the door on him. Deep inside, I felt a ferocious glowing ember of fury at Craig, the man responsible for this, who had put me in this position. But even though I hated him with so much passion, I couldn't have a man's death on my conscience forever.

Within a second I bolted to the landing and immediately shouted for my mum.

'Mum, *Mum*!' I screamed. 'It's Craig! He's overdosed, he's dying!'

My mum shot up the stairs like lightning. She looked into the room just as Kason was waking up because of my screams. I ran in, scooped him up and turned his face away from Craig's collapsed body. Mum ran over to Craig and surveyed him. She felt for a pulse and there was a slight heartbeat. I think, deep down, she probably wanted to leave him there, too – but how could she? It's just not in her nature.

She called an ambulance and within minutes I could hear the sirens blaring out up the street. I ran downstairs to open the front door and told them where he was. Two paramedics stormed into our house with a bag of equipment. I never saw what they did to

Craig and how they brought him back from the edge of death, but Mum later told me they massaged his heart, gave him the kiss of life and eventually he came round.

The ambulance men told us he nearly died from choking on his own vomit. I always thought it would have been such a poetic way for him to die because he made me feel sick constantly.

For a long time afterwards I was traumatised by what happened. In fact so were all the family. It's not something we ever speak about these days. I mean, why would we? It's not something we could ever bring up without getting really angry. I just couldn't get that image of Craig lying there in his own filth out of my head. Every time I went to sleep at night, it would flash before my eyes as if someone was throwing a movie screen up in front of me. I kept thinking, *What if Kason had been the one to wake up and see his body lying there? What if he had started playing with that filthy needle?* It makes me so angry, even now, when I think about it: a two-year-old boy, having to see his own father overdose on his bedroom floor. It's despicable.

After that happened social workers called at my mum's and basically told her if she didn't get rid of Craig, all of her children would be taken away from her. They said we weren't in a stable environment and it wasn't safe for us to be around him. Hearing that news really shook her up: that's the last thing she wanted, for all her children to be split up and taken into care. When Craig was fit and better she did the right thing and told him to leave. And without much of a fight, he did so. I don't know where he went, and I didn't care either. The only one who did care was Kason. He was pretty gutted and so he used to see Craig round at Craig's mum's house from time to time.

I hate Craig more than anyone can ever imagine. For all the times he'd stolen from us, when he let us down and was violent to us, abused us. For when he sat shivering from head to toe, his body covered in goose pimples and his brown teeth chattering. For the mental scars he's caused that will never ever heal. And because he brought that filthy drug into my home, I hate him with everything I've got.

Regan and my mum now feel the same as me, but my little brother Kason's attitude towards him is completely different. Kason idolises Craig and it's worrying to see. They spend a lot of time together and I fear that when Kason is old enough he will also take the same path as Craig did.

I get angry at Craig still because I wish he had never fallen in with that crowd and tried heroin. Our lives could have been so much different. Surely he knew the risks? But that's the problem with heroin: it doesn't matter if you're upper class or a homeless beggar on the streets, once addicted there's almost no going back. So while I say I hate Craig, at the same time I don't want anyone to ever think they're better than a drug addict because our minds tick in the same way as theirs. We have the same circuits and heroin would affect us in the same way it affects them. The same ideas that make the junkies screw up over and over would make us screw up too in their position. Most people are already addicted in some way, only not with heroin but alcohol, cigarettes, cocaine, food, steroids, plastic surgery, or something else we shouldn't be doing. We all have our vices; it's just some are more harmful than others.

My mother asked Craig one day why he had tried heroin in the first place and he couldn't give her an answer. He just said he was 'curious'. I can't understand why, when everything was good in his life – job, house, wife, kids – he would ever want to try that poison out of curiosity, so I don't sympathise with him for starting. Heroin doesn't just harm the person doing it; it harms everyone around them and ruins everyone's life in the process.

Craig is still alive, just barely, but I have nothing to do with him these days. On the brink of death, he has never been able to fully quit his drug habit. He's still stealing. Only the other month I saw he was back in court for stealing two laptops from his own mother. Unfortunately Madison and Kason are still his kids, so they kind of have a relationship with him.

Not so long ago, in September 2014, I had to pick them up from school and I saw him. When he came over to me, I hardly recognised him. I was wearing black skinny jeans, a cool white T-shirt, a leather and fur jacket, with super-high boots. My light brown hair had been blown bouncy, and I had recently purchased a pair of Céline sunglasses. It was all very Kim K and truly glamorous, like I'd just stepped off a magazine shoot. I looked a million dollars.

As he approached me, I folded my arms to make sure he knew I didn't want to chat. I looked him up and down with disgust. I can't deny the man still made me feel intimidated, but I was no longer a scared little girl. He repulsed me.

I stood up straight, squaring my shoulders, flared my nostrils and tightened my jaw. Now I was a powerful young woman and he was nothing but a maggot. How times have changed!

'How are you, Lateysha?' he asked, giving me another snapshot of those junkie brown teeth.

'Amazing,' I replied, not even bothering to ask him anything about himself.

He tried to keep the conversation flowing by telling me how when he was in prison all the other lags had sexy pictures of me on their cell walls. Like I was supposed to do cartwheels or something.

'You were in prison? What for?' I quizzed, before saying, 'Actually, I don't want to know' before he had the chance to answer.

I was just walking off when I smiled wryly and said, 'Did you hear I'm writing a book?'

'No, what about?' Craig replied.

'About my life, it's an autobiography.'

'You better not be putting anything bad about me in there!' he laughed nervously.

'Why wouldn't I? I'm going to be honest, about *everything*,' I told him, with emphasis on the word 'everything'.

'I mean it, I'm telling you, don't be putting nothing bad about me in there,' he said, a little more aggressively this time.

My eyes narrowed and I spat back, 'I'm just going to tell the truth,' before stomping off.

'Don't be saying nothing bad, alright?' he shouted after me.

Too fucking late, Craig!

Chapter Eleven

FIRST LOVE

They say there's no love like the first and I'm glad because you can't love anyone that way more than once in a lifetime. It's too hard, and it hurts too much when it ends. The first boy is always the hardest to get over, although it's a huge life lesson everyone should go through. It will be one of the worst experiences of your life, but that's just the way it is. Hold onto that; it's good experience to have and you should appreciate it, even if it pains you.

My first love was Ryan Lewis, who I met when I was fourteen. I had seen him around my campus because we both attended St Joseph's Catholic school, although that's not how we began chatting. Forget Facebook, Twitter and Instagram, back in my teenage days we used a social network called Mingleville. At the time I thought it was the coolest website ever. Basically, you uploaded a photo of yourself and people would rate you from one to five stars. The more ratings and the more stars you got, the more points you earned to spend in the Mingleville shop to update your profile.

Ryan was eighteen and a really popular guy in my school. His biological parents were from Peru, so he had that smouldering exotic look. He was adopted when he was a baby and brought up in Wales. Everyone fancied him, not just because of his good looks but because he dressed amazingly well. He always wore the latest expensive clothing and permanently had the best trainers; they were never anything but gleaming.

One afternoon I used the school computer in the ICT room and logged into my Mingleville profile. I had a notification that said, 'Ryan Lewis has rated you five stars'. When I saw it, I was ecstatic. I was giddy with excitement. Not only did Ryan Lewis know who I was, he had been on my profile and rated me five stars! The fittest lad in school thought I was hot – it was a big deal, believe me.

Of course I rated him back immediately (five stars, naturally) and soon after we began messaging. I remember as I was writing all my messages to him I was so happy. My stomach was literally filled with butterflies. Ryan only lived round the corner from my house, so the next day he asked me to walk to school with him. I was so chuffed.

The next morning, I woke up an hour early so I could make an extra-special effort with my clothes and make-up. I had on some black flared trousers, a fake white Dolce & Gabbana belt (tacky by today's standards but beyond cool back then) and I'd fashioned my tie into a big chunky knot because that was the *only* way to wear it.

As I walked out of the house to meet him, I was so nervous. He was standing at the bottom of my road and when I saw him, he floored me with his smile. It unnerved me and I had to look away out of embarrassment. I couldn't ever remember feeling that way before. He was a total stranger and yet I felt such a strong connection to him.

After that, we walked to school together every day. It was so innocent and cute. He would carry my school bag and we would talk about all sorts. We would literally chat away for hours – about people we knew, about fashion, music, our families, anything. It was all so easy and relaxed. Everyone in school was jealous. They used to say, 'Why the fuck is Ryan walking to school with Lateysha?' I suppose they thought it was weird because of the age difference. After all, he was four years older than me and he was this über-cool, popular guy, whereas I was just a kid.

Don't get me wrong, I wasn't some sort of geek no one wanted to hang around with. I was popular too, in my year, but I wasn't the prettiest girl by a long stretch. I think that's why people thought our friendship was strange because he could literally have bagged any girl he wanted, but he chose me. I didn't think it was strange, though – no one knew the connection we had and after only a week of knowing Ryan, I could feel myself falling for him.

I literally worshipped the ground he walked on and thought he was amazing in every way. I'm sure everyone has felt the same at some point. Think back to the time when you first really fancied a guy; you'll know what I mean. Someone older was showing me attention and I loved it. I loved that he liked me – well, at the time I wasn't sure if he did, but why would he rate me five stars on Mingleville if he didn't?

At first, he wouldn't let me tell anyone about us. I think he was nervous of the reaction because of the age difference, him being in the sixth form and me only in the third year. But one night he asked me to go for a drink round the local park. I know, classy, right? He brought with him a bottle of wine and we drank it on a park bench while listening to music on his phone. It sounds like nothing but at that point I was so young, so naïve, so foolish – this was *the* most amazing date I'd ever been on. In fact, it was the *only* date so far! We lay down on the grass, staring at the stars. Actually, it was really romantic and right then there was no place I would rather have been. I just knew from that moment on, I was head over heels in love.

Not long after that night we started seeing each other officially. He asked me out over a text and it was the best feeling I'd ever had. He was my best friend and now he was my boyfriend. We were extremely close and I felt like I could confide in him about my situation at home. It took me a few months, but then I revealed the darker side of my life: about Craig and the overdose, the shit I'd been through with my dad. About the time I tried to kill myself. I made myself totally vulnerable to this guy.

Now I know this sounds stupid, but I felt as if Ryan, in some way, was sent to protect me. Not that I want to get spiritual, but the only way I can describe him was as a saviour. He helped me in a way he never knew. We became inseparable and did everything together. Best friends, we were like brother and sister and lovers all in one. I know it might seem daft saying this because we were so young and you might conclude I wouldn't know what love felt like at that age but I had never felt so strongly for another person. I'd been constantly let down by the men in my life, but Ryan was the only one who was different.

He introduced me to his family quite early on and I treated them like they were my own. They made me feel welcome and after only a month, I was basically living at his place because I loved spending time with him. I remember back then feeling like I was on Cloud Nine. But when you love someone that much, so much that it consumes you, something has to give. My whole focus was Ryan. Distracted by him, I began skipping class. I never did any of the homework and was falling behind badly. Ryan had now left the sixth form and was working at an accountants firm. It was because I knew I would never get to see him at school that I didn't want to go. He would urge me to go while he was at work, but I wouldn't. Instead I would wait for him to get back home at his house, either lying about going into school or if he asked me, I would distract him with sex.

Before Ryan, I'd never been with anyone before. He took my virginity when I was fifteen. I know I was underage, but we didn't care at the time. I felt like I was ready and I never regret doing it for a second because I was deeply in love. I was really nervous at first, I had no idea what I was doing, but Ryan really put me at ease. Yes, it was painful like it is for most first-timers, but in all honesty I was glad to get it out of the way, and it really brought mine and Ryan's relationship closer. After that, our sex life was, to put it mildly, incredible. We were so passionate with one another. If you ask me, it's the only way to be. As far as I'm concerned, unless it's mad, passionate, extraordinary love, it's a total waste of time. And ours definitely wasn't that. Like I said, it was all-consuming. I couldn't focus on anything else. My school attendance, especially during GCSEs, was pathetic. I was never going to class, so I wasn't getting the work I needed to revise. When I had to sit my exams, I sat there sweating, knowing failure was the only option. I left school with one GCSE in English and all the rest were Ds, Es and Us. It was embarrassing, but I reasoned I had my saviour: my Ryan. Everything would be all right. My mum never really knew the extent of my truancy; she would just see me leave the house in my uniform and assume I was going to go in. She never really asked me how I was getting on with my exams either, so I never told her. Or if she did, I would just say, 'I'm doing the best I can mum.'

In hindsight, I do regret the way I was when I was younger. I wish I'd had more motivation to want to do well at school. I wish I'd had a parent that was more forceful with me, too. Not that I'm slating my mum or anything, she was doing all she could for me, but I never felt that I had anyone to make proud. My mum was always busy with my siblings, Dad didn't care, my grandparents weren't on the scene, who else was there? Did anyone care if I got all As or never sat my exams at all? No. The outcome was always going to be the same, regardless of what my results were.

But back to Ryan. Ryan treated me like a princess. We would be constantly shopping in Birmingham or Bristol and he would always treat me. He liked to dress me and because he had such good fashion sense, he thought he knew what looked better on me than I did. He would pick out my clothes and tell me what to wear. At first, my mum and my brother Regan were dubious because he was so much older than me. In fact, the term they used was 'disgusting perv', but in the end, when they gave him a chance, they really liked him. They thought he was a great influence on me and they could see how well he treated me.

Like I said before, I got extremely close to Ryan's family. His mother, father and sister were just like an extension of my own family. Our relationship was the best and I had never been happier in my whole life. But isn't that just the way, that when everything seems to be going well, there's a big storm brewing somewhere?

It was the most heartbreaking and terrible tragedy. When I was fifteen, Ryan's mother died. It was so unexpected that we were all at a complete loss. At the time she was quite ill. She'd been prescribed some pills by the doctor and accidentally overdosed. I still remember the day when he called me in floods of tears and broke the devastating news that his mother had just died. It was so shocking and I didn't know how to react. I was completely and utterly heartbroken, for Ryan and his family. It was such a tremendous loss. Immediately, I shot round to see him and he just collapsed in floods of tears in my arms.

She had died in her bedroom that morning. Ryan had found her and I can't begin to imagine what that must have been like. When I got round to his house he asked me to go in the bedroom to see her. I had never had to deal with anything like that in my life and to be honest, I didn't know if I could. All I knew was I had to be strong for Ryan and to do as he wished. As I walked into the bedroom, I saw her lying there so peacefully, with paramedics around her. She was an amazing woman and I couldn't believe this was happening. The last time I'd seen her she had been laughing along with us and now she was morbidly still. I'd never seen a body before and it was even worse seeing someone I cared about with the life ebbed out of them. My heart broke for Ryan and it still does every day when I think about it. Whatever has gone on between us since, I'll never hate him or wish him ill will – we have been through too much together.

It was the most horrible time of my life. I don't think Ryan knew how to deal with it. Besides, how could he? There's no handbook on that sort of thing. I suppose he just did whatever he felt he needed to do. The night after his mum's funeral he went out with the boys, even though I advised him against it. I didn't want him to do anything stupid and I prayed he wouldn't push me away. He had been my saviour and I felt now it was my turn to repay the favour, if only he would let me. But when he went out, he didn't contact me at all and I was so worried about him. I had a bad butterfly feeling in the pit of my stomach and I prayed he was going to be all right when I next saw him.

It wasn't until two days later that he reappeared. I was at my mum's and he walked past the window and sheepishly knocked on the door. I was absolutely fuming. Now, I know that sounds selfish, but he needed to grieve, not be going out with his mates. I was trying to help and he completely threw it back in my face. He came round all apologetic and of course I completely understood. I couldn't be mad at him, not when he was hurting so badly. Anyway, I knew he was sorry – he even offered to buy me a puppy to make up for his disappearing act – but I didn't want presents, I just wanted to comfort him in his hour of need.

It was only recently that I found out why he was acting so guilty and what he had actually been doing on those two days. One of his friends told me that the night after his mum's funeral he had visited a brothel and slept with two prostitutes. I didn't want to believe it. How *could* he? It makes me physically ill to think of it now. I understand his mind must have been all over the place, but really, is there any excuse for meaningless sex? I was so disappointed in him; I don't understand how anyone could do that to someone who loves them beyond words. To me, it's incomprehensible.

After that, our relationship was in freefall. Sometimes a heartbreaking event can bring two people together, other times it can rip you apart, and in our case it was definitely the latter. He was going out constantly. There were cheating rumours going around our friends and although I didn't want to believe it, deep down, I knew it must be true. Honestly, about five girls claimed to have been with him behind my back. I dismissed them all and put them out of my mind, but I knew there was no smoke without fire.

One time I went over to his house and he was sporting a fresh black eye. When I asked where it came from, he told me he had fallen over when he was drunk and hit his head. About half an hour later, he was messing around on his computer and a Facebook message popped up from a girl called Lois, his best friend's sister. The message said, 'Did I leave my phone in your room last night?'

As soon as I saw that, I felt a sharp stab in my gut and my heart started beating fast. I asked him what it was all about and what Lois had been doing round his house. Instantly, he began flapping and displayed all the signs of a complete liar. He told me he'd had a party, that she must have gone to his room and just happened to leave her phone in there. Yeah, right!

Immediately, I screamed at him and then broke down in tears. 'I can't believe you slept with her!' I sobbed uncontrollably. I was crying so hard, I could barely catch my breath. Obviously, he denied it completely, but I knew he had done it: the guilt was written all over his face. Immediately, I messaged her – I just wanted the truth. She knew I was with Ryan and I would rather have known if he had shagged her so I could end things with him. I said, 'Lois, how did you come to leave your phone in Ryan's room?' And she heartlessly replied, 'Ask your boyfriend, babe.'

There it was again, that sharp stab of pain in my gut and I collapsed, weeping. Ryan tried to weasel his way out of it, but then I started to look for clues. I went in his shed – I say 'shed' but it was more like a den for all of us to hang out in. On the wall it used to say, 'Ryan loves Lateysha', but Lois had sprayed over it and written, 'Ryan loves Lois'. As if I didn't need more ammunition.

I heard rumours of what actually went down and it went like this: Ryan had slept with Lois in his bedroom during the party. His best friend (her brother) had walked in on them, punched Ryan in the face, which is why he had a black eye, and dragged his sister out by the hair, which is why she had left her phone. Even though I knew what was the truth, I didn't want to believe it. I just kept thinking he wouldn't do that to me. I chose to look the other way because I was deeply in love with the guy. Love makes you blind, I suppose.

Afterwards, I became terribly insecure. I began questioning

everything about myself and my self-esteem was at an all-time low. Maybe I should have discussed how I was feeling but I never really opened up to anyone, although everyone noticed a change in my attitude. I was miserable and would be moping around all the time. The odd time over a cuppa my mum would ask me what was the matter and I would say I'd argued with Ryan. She was really good and sympathetic about it; she knew I loved Ryan and that telling me to 'split up with him' was not the answer. Instead she listened and tried to make me feel good about myself by telling me how beautiful I was, what a good, kind heart I had and that he would be a fool to get rid of me, which was probably not true, but really sweet of her.

To put it mildly, our relationship was in turmoil. We began arguing and fighting, like you wouldn't believe. I remember one time throwing a vase at him and it only just missed his head. He would drag me down the stairs by my hair. All we ever did was fight and accuse each other of shit. It should have ended then, but we muddled on for far too long.

When I was seventeen, things went from bad to worse. I was working in a salon called Flawless just after I was kicked out of school for doing that amazing striptease. Remember, I told you about that, right at the start? Ryan's life was fast going off the rails and so, in turn, was mine. He had begun dealing Mephedrone (coined 'meow meow' or 'M-cat' by the kids who used it). It's a drug that produces similar effects to Ecstasy, amphetamines or cocaine. Back then, the drug was legal, but it was also very dangerous and highly addictive. All our mates were on it and even more so now that Ryan was peddling it. He was also using it himself, which made me uncomfortable. He knew my past experiences with drugs because of the shit I'd been put through with Craig, but he would tell me it was completely different and

I believed him. In a way I could see what he was saying: it was acceptable to try M-cat, it was legal and it was supposed to be harmless, whereas heroin is regarded as a dirty scumbag drug only used by the down-and-outs to get them through their shitty lives. It was this reasoning that made me think it was OK to try it, too, and the more I had it, the more I forgot about my former hatred of drugs, because to me they weren't in the same league.

His dad would go on long holidays to Thailand, leaving Ryan in charge of the house. But Ryan would abuse that trust and no sooner was his father out of the country than he would throw a massive house party. Those nights were crazy, when I think back. Everyone would be drinking, smoking, shagging and getting off their faces.

In the space of a couple of months I went from a size 10 to a size 6. I was so skinny because all I was doing was sniffing drugs, which curbed my appetite completely. It became relentless; I was addicted to it. Even if I tried to stop it, I couldn't because all my friends were doing it and my boyfriend was dealing, so it was constantly around me.

I remember many people commenting on my weight loss at the time and I would lie by saying I had taken up running. My boss from the salon was suspicious but she never pushed me on the subject, something I was glad about. I didn't want to admit what I was doing, even to myself. She knew I wasn't exercising. Yeah, I had lost weight but I'd never looked so terrible in all my life. My eyes were constantly glazed and black, my skin was always spotty and I was completely zoned out. Back then, I was desperately unhappy: moody, miserable and continually on a comedown. I wanted to stop doing the drugs, I really did. Every Monday morning after a heavy weekend, I would hit rock bottom, sinking into a deep despair. I would assess my whole life and honestly think to myself, why am I on this planet?

If you have anything bad going on in your life, I advise you never to do drugs. They will make you feel good for a few hours while you're feeling the effects, but what comes up must surely come down. And when you start to feel that comedown, what seems bad before will seem a thousand times worse. It was at these times I would start to think of Craig and how what I was doing was no better than what he used to do. If my mum had ever known at the time she would have absolutely battered me, I'm sure. It was a really stupid thing to do and, yes, I suppose these days I do regret doing it. Maybe that's why my attention span is bad and my memory is shot to pieces. I had no clue how these drugs were affecting my brain and after the small initial high, they just made you feel terrible. I urge you all not to try it, because honestly, it's really pathetic.

I'd complained to Ryan over and over about how depressed I was. I needed to get away and he agreed I could use a break, so he kindly paid for me to go to Magaluf with my friends. To be honest, I think it was the guilt of him cheating on me that made him pay. He knew I hadn't deserved the way he treated me although he also probably used it as the perfect chance to cheat on me some more, while I was out the country. But two can play at that game.

While on holiday, I had an amazing time and I was delighted to be away from everything back in Wales. Not many people go to Magaluf and find it more therapeutic than home, do they? But that just goes to show how fucked up my life in Port Talbot was.

One night on the strip I met this incredible eighteen-year-old guy from London, who was drop-dead gorgeous with a wicked personality. He looked like the rapper Nelly (which, by the way, is *just* my type). I fancied him something chronic. Now, I knew the feelings I had for this boy weren't normal and if I was completely happy in my relationship with Ryan, I wouldn't be lusting after him so much. I suppose it confirmed what I already knew: that we needed to split up sooner rather than later.

My feelings were so strong for this hunk that after a few days of getting to know him, I found myself cheating on Ryan. It was only a kiss but still, I shouldn't have wanted to kiss other guys if I was happy with my boyfriend.

I didn't know if it was the sun, the sea or the Sangria, but I think I actually fell for him a little bit. When I had to leave him and get back on the plane to Wales, I cried. Back to my shitty life in Port Talbot, with a guy who didn't love me, and who I was rapidly falling out of love with too. I made a vow to myself to let things fizzle out with Ryan when I returned home. This would be the easiest thing to help us both move on and would cushion the blow of a break-up, I thought. It would take a few months, but it was the best option available. Of course, I would miss Ryan; he was my safety net, but we weren't happy anymore and the arguments were becoming unbearable. There were more bad days than good ones.

All I could think about was my holiday romance guy and how I needed to see him again. We had swapped numbers and about a week after I returned home, he messaged me inviting me down to his birthday party in London.

I grabbed three of my friends and we drove down to London for the bash. He'd spared no expense and even gone so far as to hire a limo. I was absolutely delighted to be with him again and I got this mad rush of feelings for him. It was pure unadulterated lust and I couldn't contain myself around him. And as you can probably guess, it wasn't long before we were climbing the stairs to his bedroom and embroiled in a steamy session of passion. The lights were off when we were having sex, which didn't matter to me. Sensual and seductive, it was just the way I liked it.

In the morning I woke up with my head on his chest and we cuddled sweetly, although I was hungover like you wouldn't believe. My eyes were burning, my throat as dry as the desert and my head pounding. Kindly, he rose from the bed to get me a glass of water, which was more than Ryan would do for me in those days. If Ryan had a hangover, he would just lie in his pit until the next evening, order up a pizza and fall back asleep again, completely ignoring me for the entire day. But this guy quite happily trundled off to the kitchen to get me some water to quench my thirst.

How sweet of him, I thought.

I heard him coming back into the bedroom and I made myself look as sexy as possible by just wrapping a sheet around my body. But when he walked towards me, in full daylight with his top off, I saw something that made me want to burst out laughing.

This sounds really mean to say, but the guy had one bitch tit. I kid you not: he had one massive right moob! As soon as I'd clocked it, I couldn't take my eyes off it. He could see me staring at it and actually said, 'Ignore my bitch tit! I'm having surgery on it. It came when I hit puberty.'

Now he had said it out loud, it wasn't like I could just forget about it. He'd made me even more aware of it, to the point where I felt I had to address it. 'Oh really? Why you having surgery, you can't even see it.' What a big fat fucking lie! It was unbelievable. His banger was like a C-cup, while the other one was completely flat. I was dying to laugh.

The worst part was when he got back into bed, he attempted to get all amorous again. I tried to say I felt ill from my hangover, but he just kept jabbing his knob into me until eventually I gave in. He climbed on top of me and in the cold light of day I could see his moob jiggling around. I felt sick, but like a car crash on the motorway, I couldn't take my eyes off it. There it was, shaking around, while he pounded me. I kept thinking, *How the fuck had I not noticed his nork before now?* I suppose all the baggy clothes did wonders for concealing his chest.

Suffice to say, it was the last I saw of 'Breast Boy' although it wasn't the last time I got to hear about him. About a week later, one of my so-called friends told Ryan I had gone to London and cheated on him. Obviously, he was fuming and lashed out at me, physically, and slapped me across the face. I knew what he had done was wrong, but then again so was I, so I reasoned our actions cancelled each other out. Since I couldn't defend myself against the accusation I had to admit it to him. He was gutted, but then again, look at all the times he'd cheated on me. There were accusations flying around weekly by now. And so we vowed to work on our relationship and instead of letting things fizzle out, like they should have done, we tried again.

Maybe if Ryan and me hadn't cheated on each other we could have worked, but I don't know. I suppose we were just too young. If we'd met when we were thirty, who knows? But life ain't that easy.

Not long after my cheating revelation I agreed to move in with him, hoping this might cement our relationship. There was another reason too: his dad had thrown him out. He was sick of all the parties and told Ryan to pack his bags, so he came to live at my house with my mum and we were sharing a bedroom with my two little sisters, Paris and Madison, which was obviously less than ideal.

The worst part was Ryan would piss me off all the time by disappearing. I would wake up in the middle of the night and he would be gone, just like that. He would vanish. I'd call him, demanding to know where he was, and he would answer his phone, saying he was at a party somewhere. I couldn't believe he would just wake up and go to a party while I was sleeping. He wouldn't come home for days because he knew if he returned and he was fucked from all the drugs he was taking, I would freak. He became a classic work-all-week, party-all-weekend guy. Come Monday morning he was screwed, but unbelievably he was still managing to hold down a job.

By now, Ryan had moved from meow meow to getting off his face on ketamine, a powerful general anaesthetic mainly used as a horse tranquilliser. It makes you feel like everything is going in slow motion. I should know – I tried it once and never again. It made me feel like I was floating and literally slowed all the workings of my brain down. It was like my world was in slow motion and I didn't enjoy the feeling at all. Eventually, Ryan would come home, all apologetic, and weasel his way around me. I didn't want to see him on the streets, so eventually I would forgive him.

Meanwhile, my mum was sick of all the arguments and the drama that came with our relationship. It wasn't good for my siblings to see us at each other's throats all the time either. She wanted us both out and so we had to find somewhere to live, which is why I agreed to go with him. We found a nice little house in a place called Skewen, twenty minutes from where I grew up. I thought maybe the move could be a fresh start, but of course things never improved. We continued to argue the whole time and I was becoming more miserable by the day. I didn't particularly want to move in with Ryan, but I felt I was left with no choice and now I hated my life with him more than ever.

Once again I was trapped, a prisoner in my own home.

Chapter Twelve

FISTICUFFS

I stayed round at my mum's house one night because Ryan and me had another screaming row. They were happening all too frequently now and something had to change soon. I wanted to end the relationship, but he was my safety blanket. At times, he'd been the only stability in my life. I had a major fear about standing on my own two feet and that's why I was reluctant to end it, but I decided that evening we should have a serious talk and decide where we both saw our futures, because we were screwing up our lives.

Leaving Mum's house the next morning, I stepped out of the front door and gazed at my car. I had a beautiful blue Mini and to my horror, someone had vandalised it. The door panels had been scratched and the windscreen was egged.

'What the *fuck*?' I screamed.

'What's up, 'Teesh?' my mum called from the house.

'Look at my car! It's been trashed! Who would do this?' I fumed.

'Maybe it's just kids. Don't worry, get it cleaned and it will be OK,' she yelled back.

'That's not the point. Why would they do this to my car and no one else's?' I was tamping!

Something in my gut told me it wasn't kids. Whoever had done it had meant to do this to me. But I couldn't understand why. As far as I was concerned, I had no enemies, I was living a relatively quiet life, living with Ryan, going out with my friends and keeping myself to myself. Why would anyone be so evil? I loved my car so much; it was my pride and joy. To me this was quite clearly an intentional attack and they had hit me where it hurt.

Still fuming, I cleaned up the mess and went to work. By this time I had left work at the hair salon; I was sick of the monotony of sweeping up hair all day and had decided to move to an energy company, SA12 Energy Services, where I was doing all the boring admin jobs, which I also hated. I had gone from the frying pan into the fire, so to speak. The company was fairly small and I wasn't on much money. After tax, I was only earning round £700 a month, even though I worked all the hours I could. It was a 9am–6pm office job, five days a week and it was soul-destroying.

I figured I'd never be able to find out who had done it, so I wasn't going to waste any more of my time thinking about the sad loser. That was until a week later when some guy I knew called Luke told me who'd attacked my car. I don't know how he knew, but he was right and he confessed it was a girl called Paige Harris. When he told me, it made sense. I knew of the girl, we had been mates at one time, but I didn't know what I had done to upset her. Funnily enough, the last time I'd seen her at a party she had been asking me all about my car. She'd waltzed up and said, 'Have you got a Mini?' in her squeaky Welsh voice.

'Yeah, a blue one,' I'd replied.

'Oh, that's so cool! I'd love one. How do you afford that?' she'd quizzed.

It was a big deal for me to have a Mini at eighteen where I come from and all the girls in my area were extremely jealous. It was expensive but, generously, Ryan had paid for the deposit and I paid all the monthly bills with my income from work.

Of course I was furious when I found out it was Paige who had done the deed, but I wasn't hell bent on revenge or I would have called her out as soon as I learned it was her. Instead I just pitied her and got on with my life.

That was until I was in Revolution in Swansea. I'd been in there a couple of hours and by this point, I was well oiled. I was with my pals Casey, Harrison and Ellis, another friend from school. We had pre-drinks at Harrison's first and then went straight on to Revolution. Out the corner of my eye I saw Paige Harris and her friends, standing at the bar. I asked my friends what they thought I should do, go and confront her about my car or just leave it? They all agreed I should speak to Paige. With hindsight, I admit, it wasn't the best place to do it, but like I said, my judgement was clouded by alcohol. I walked over to her, tapped her lightly on the shoulder to attract her attention and just came right out with it.

'Paige, why did you egg my car?' I asked.

'What you on about?' she said.

'Why did you egg my car?' I repeated, a little louder this time.

'What?' she scowled. 'I fucking didn't, you stupid bitch!'

Whoa, calm down, I thought, *there was no need for that reaction.*

'Paige, you did! Luke told me, don't deny it,' I said, choosing to ignore her 'stupid bitch' comment.

'Oh, fuck off, you fucking black slut!' she told me. And in one swift motion, she pushed me almost to the point of me falling over.

That was it – I wasn't going to let her get away with calling me that. Absolutely raging now, I pushed her back. Before I knew it, we ended up in a fight where we were both pushing and shoving each other around. The next thing I knew, she was pulling my hair down and somehow she ended up on top of me on the floor. She had her nails digging into my eye sockets as hard as she could and I just remember being in agony and thinking, *How am I going to get out of this?*

I sunk my teeth into her leg and bit her until she screamed, but still she didn't let me go. I bit her arm slightly too, although not hard. It was only for a few seconds – I just wanted to get her off me.

Eventually the bouncers came over, pulled us apart and threw Paige out of the front door while one of them threw me out the back door, where my friends rushed to meet me.

It all happened so fast, my friends were in total shock and so was I. My eyes were hurting where she'd scratched me. My hair had been pulled out in chunks, my extensions were ripped out and I looked a complete state.

Really upset, I called Ryan and asked him to come and pick me up. Even though we had our arguments, he always had my back when I needed him. But while I was waiting for him, I bumped into Paige and her pals outside again. We got into another slanging match, with both of us screaming profanities at each other until my friends took me away from the situation.

Ryan arrived shortly afterwards and I spent the whole journey back to Port Talbot filling him in on what had happened.

'You look like shit,' he told me, as I swung my legs into the car.

'Thanks, love you too,' I said sarcastically.

'I'm playing. What's happened? Are you OK?'

'We had a fight.'

'Who did?'

'Paige Harris and me – I asked that stupid bitch why she wrecked my car and then she attacked me, called me a black slut and all sorts. Oh, Ryan, it was awful!' I raged.

I was still so angry, I couldn't believe how all this had happened.

'God, 'Tesha! Are you OK? Are you hurt?'

'She hit me, pulled my hair, scratched my eyes,' I said, showing him the marks on my face. 'I can hardly see anything, my eyes are killing me, what the fuck is her problem?'

'Did your friends not stop it?' he asked.

'They were over the other side of the bar. It all happened so fast. The bouncers pulled her off and slung us both out. She started it all,' I protested.

That night I went home to bed and tried to forget all about Paige. I wasn't out for a revenge attack, as far as I was concerned it was done. I hated her and she hated me, but that was it. Over.

When I woke up the next day, I saw what she'd written about me on Facebook. I can't remember her exact words but she said something along the lines of, 'Lateysha the fucking dog bit me last night. I had to go and get a tetanus shot because she bit me with those doggy teeth.'

It wasn't just her, either. Her mum and all her mates started piping up, slagging me off and making out I had attacked Paige. My mum wasn't like hers, she wasn't one to get involved with all the Facebook drama, but my brother Regan stuck up for me and so did some of my friends.

Maybe it's just me, but I just kept thinking, why would you announce to the world about fighting with another girl? It's not something to be proud of; it's embarrassing. I was deeply ashamed of what had happened but it was almost like she was revelling in it, which I found totally weird. But since she had slagged me off, I took to my page to slag her right back. It was completely childish,

I get that now, but at the time I was so angry. The thing that pissed me off the most was why she had a problem with me in the first place. She was obviously jealous of me, or at least my lovely little car, and couldn't handle the fact I had something she didn't.

Meanwhile, I was in a severe amount of pain. Paige had ripped huge chunks out of my hair and I had brutal tears on my scalp. Later that day, I went to the doctor's and after a quick examination, they gave me strong painkillers. My eyes were still hurting too. It was like I had blurred vision constantly. At work I struggled to see my computer and I found it difficult to read road signs when I was driving, but I reasoned I'd live. All I could do now was try to forget.

About a month later, I was on the set of a music video in Swansea. I knew a lady called Dawn, who was a talent agent. She was organising a music video for a rapper called Dretonio and asked if I'd be in the video. I was absolutely buzzing because I was to be the lead female on the shoot, the one who got the most screen time and the best close-up shots. I'd never done anything like this before and couldn't wait to get on set to strut my stuff. I only got paid about £80, but I got to keep the dress I was going to wear, which was absolutely stunning. Short and white, it was a barely-there garment, which was backless and cut really low at the front. Totally hoochy mama!

Scrolling through my phone while a hairdresser wanded my hair in sections, I received a message from Ryan, which read 'Call me now!'

I told the hairdresser I needed to make a quick phone call and so she busied herself with one of the other girl's hair. Dialling

Ryan's number, I half-expected him to be asking me where his shoes were or something equally unimportant.

'Ryan, what's wrong? I'm really busy,' I sighed, annoyed at the interruption.

''Teesh, the police have been round to your mum's house!'

'*What?*' I shrieked.

'They're arresting you because of the fight with Paige!' he told me.

'Are you serious?' I said, before bursting into tears.

'I told them you were down in Swansea and they are going to try and find you there. Just come back home now.'

'Why did you tell them that? What should I do?' I said. My hands were shaking as I tried to keep the phone next to my ear.

'I had to; they made me. When you weren't at your mum's, your mum called me to see if I was with you.'

'OK,' I said. 'I'm leaving now.'

After I ended the call, I burst out crying again in the midst of this glamorous music video set. Everyone around me was so concerned but when I explained the situation, they had no choice but to find another girl for the video. To be honest, I was truly gutted but what choice did I have? I couldn't believe Paige had actually gone to the police over a stupid fight, which she had started and which happened over a month ago. It was insane.

Grabbing my things, I bolted for the door, hurried down the noisy metal stairwell, out into the car park, and ran over to my Mini. It was then that I saw out of my peripheral vision a fluorescent car pulling up at the side of me. Before I knew it, two policemen then jumped out in front of me.

'Are you Lateysha Henry?' one of them asked.

Fuck! Was this really happening? I just froze and felt sick. I couldn't even speak, so I simply nodded my head.

'Lateysha Henry, I am arresting you on suspicion of the assault of Paige Harris. You do not have to say anything but it may harm your defence if you do not mention when questioned something you later rely on in court. Anything you do say may be given in evidence.'

I was stunned. It was like I was in a real-life episode of *The Bill*. I wanted the ground to open up and swallow me whole. The shorter of the two officers unleashed his cuffs from his belt and went to try and restrain me.

'No, please. Don't cuff me!' I wept, as the tears rolled down my face. 'Let me drive my car to the station, you can follow behind me.' The two men looked at each other. After deciding I probably wasn't going to run away, they let me drive my Mini.

When I got to Swansea police station, I was terrified. I couldn't stop shaking. It was exactly like you see on the TV. They made me sign in, took my fingerprints and then made me stand there holding a sign while they photographed my face for the mug shots.

Next, they took all my clothes including my shoes and instead gave me white overalls to wear, like I was about to go out painting. Then they escorted me to a cell. As I looked around the grey box room I could hear nothing but clanging noises and footsteps in the corridors. Rocking backwards and forwards, I cried and cried. All I could do was think, *How have I ended up here? Is this what my life has become? Sat in a dank and dirty prison cell?*

Nine hours I waited until they were finally ready to conduct my police interview. By this point I was just so happy to be getting out of that freezing cold cell, I didn't care that I was about to be interrogated.

A robust-looking woman with short dark hair came in, parked herself in front of me and gave me a stern look. Already she was a total bitch and she hadn't even opened her mouth. There was another officer in the room, sitting on her right-hand side, who was operating the tape machine. When they were ready to record, she began laying into me. On and on she went with her bullish accusations.

'So you hit her first, didn't you, Lateysha? You were upset about what you thought Paige had done to your car and you hit her first.'

'No, I didn't,' I kept repeating. 'I did not hit her first.'

'Paige had done nothing to you and you hit her.'

'Why are you making out she is the victim?' I pleaded. 'It was *me*, she hit *me* – all I did was ask her why she did that to my car!'

'Lateysha, you're lying, aren't you?'

'No, I am not,' I said and out of frustration, I began to cry.

'What about this then?' she said, as she handed over photos of Paige's leg. Granted there was a small bite mark, but I hadn't drawn blood. I just bit hard enough that she would get off me – I never intended to cause any long-lasting damage.

Tears were rolling down my face, I was wiping my nose on the back of my sleeve and my body was shuddering because I was crying so hard.

'I want a solicitor. This isn't fair, I didn't hit her first,' I said.

They stopped the interview while they phoned me a duty solicitor. They had offered me one when I first got to the station but I didn't think I needed one at first. I had no idea I was going to be questioned so aggressively. On arrival, he sat me down in a different interview room and I told him exactly what had happened that night in Revolution. Later, when they re-interviewed me, my solicitor stepped in to back my corner many times so they couldn't be so harsh with their questioning. I was so glad he was there but I still couldn't believe I was in this situation. I kept looking upwards and thinking, this is not my life.

Eventually I was released on bail and they allowed me to go home. When I was given back all my clothes and belongings, Ryan was sitting in reception and I was so happy to see him. He had driven there as soon as he knew I was about to be arrested and waited eleven hours for me to be released. I broke down in tears again for the hundredth time that day and told him just to hug me tightly. Despite everything we had put each other through, when it mattered he was there for me.

Life continued as normal for a little while. I went back to work, kept my head down and tried to forget all about what had happened with Paige until one afternoon when my solicitor phoned to tell me I had been charged with assault. At first I thought the whole episode was going to be dropped by the police, but I wasn't so lucky. I considered the whole thing to be ridiculous. Don't get me wrong, we should never have come to blows, but to take it this far and charge me with assault when I had done nothing to start the scrap was crazy.

My solicitor explained everything to me. He gave me a court date and told me I would have to stand in front of three magistrates for a plea hearing. I discussed my options with him and he agreed the best course of action would be to plead 'not guilty' because I genuinely hadn't started the fight with her. Yes, I confronted her and yes, I did bite her, but I only bit her out of self-defence and with that in mind, I agreed I wasn't going to admit to something I hadn't done.

Chapter Thirteen

LONDON TOWN

y mum says I'm stupidly fearless. Or was that stupid and
fearless? I can never remember. But she's right in the way
that I take big risks and often get myself into mad situations. One
such occasion was just after I'd had that fight with Paige. A few
of my friends and me decided to swerve going out in Wales for a
while, to let the dust settle and try pastures new.

I can't remember which one of us decided the city, but when
London was suggested we all jumped on the idea. I took it upon
myself to book the hotel room and said they could all pay me
back when we got there.

When the weekend came round, all the girls – Kim, Lindsay,
Zoe and Letitia – piled into my Mini and I began the three-hour
long journey to the capital. We arrived at our chosen destination,
the Holiday Inn Express in Hammersmith, rocked up to reception
and gave the Russian beauty on the counter our booking details.
Surprisingly, or unsurprisingly if you know what I'm like, I had

messed up the booking in classic Lateysha fashion. To most of those who know me it's a wonder how I get through life and travel all over the world – I can be a proper ditz at times!

On arrival they said I had no reservation because me, being the idiot I am, had booked the room for the next month and they had no other availability. Luckily, my friends saw the funny side. It was late already, far too late to start hunting round for another hotel, so we resigned ourselves to getting ready in my little blue Mini, which was a struggle. Have you ever tried to get a bandage dress on in a small car? Or attempted to do your make-up in a rear-view mirror? Trust me, it ain't easy!

We made the most of a bad situation and also had to accept the fact we would be sleeping in the car later. Ridiculous, I know, but we had no other option. We could have booked another, more expensive hotel room but we wanted to keep our cash for our night out. I mean have you seen the price of drinks in London?

That evening we headed to DSTRKT in the West End, which is one of my favourite London clubs. We did our usual lap around the club and it didn't take us long to get chatting to some black guys and they invited us to their table for the evening to party with them. I say 'party', but we basically nailed all their alcohol within a couple of hours before they asked us back to their 'plush penthouse' somewhere in London. All night, they'd been telling us how one of them had this gorgeous flat, where we could all hang until we sobered up. We had nowhere else to go, these guys seemed cool, and without further thought, we decided to go home with them.

A huge minibus arrived outside the club to take us back to their place. I hadn't a clue where we were headed and after about thirty minutes of being in the minibus, we still hadn't arrived even though they had said their place was round the corner. Weird. I

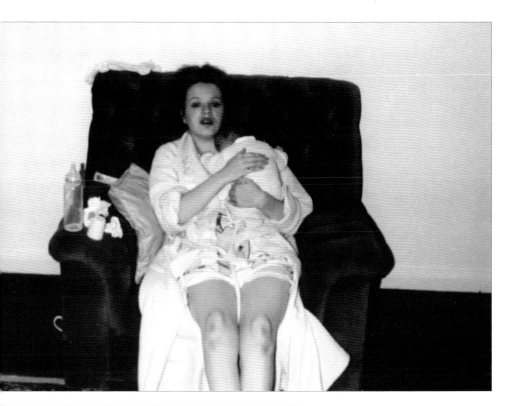

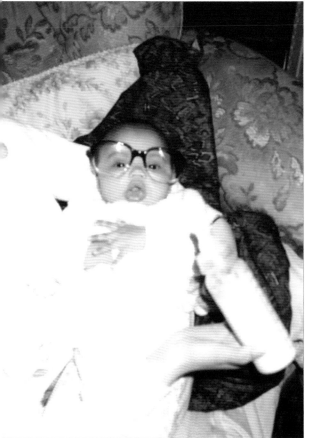

Above: My mum Debbie and me only a few days after I was born.

Below: I was always a poser from an early age.

Above left: Giving my grandpa Michael a shave.

Above right: Some things never change, I still love to pamper myself in the bath for hours on end.

Below left: Getting behind the wheel for the first time!

Below right: Me and Regan in our first school photograph.

Above: Practicing for my singing career. I really thought I was going to be a superstar back then.

Below: My brother Regan showing off his muscles.

Above: My stepdad with me, Regan and Paris.

Below: Me, Regan and little Paris.

Above left: In high school before I got kicked out for lap dancing. That's the same tie I used in my strip tease.

Above right: Me and my first love Ryan Lewis on holiday in Greece.

Above: On holiday with my best friends in Magaluf. (From left to right) Me, Harrison, Jayde, Casey, Niamh, Roxanne and Ellis.

Below left: At my best friend Casey's birthday surrounded by friends in Giovanni's Cardiff. (From left to right, top to bottom) Niamh, Harrison, Casey, Ellis, Nicola, Myself, Nicole and Lina.

Above left: All my brothers and sisters on Paris's prom. There's me, Regan, Paris, Kason and Madison.

Above right: My current boyfriend Ben. He's the love of my life.

Below left: That infamous night with Amir Khan.

Below right: On the set of Ne-Yo's music video with Nadia, Erin and Ne-Yo.

Above: All *The Valleys* girls at the National Television awards.

© *PA Images*

Below: Me and D-Jukes on the set of our music video 'You Beautiful'.

Modelling in my favourite place in the whole world, Miami.

was getting nervous, but what else could we do? It would have taken us forever to get back to the car. I didn't even know where we were.

Eventually, after another ten minutes, the car finally pulled up at what can only be described as a ghetto. My pal Kim kept saying, 'I thought you lived in a penthouse?' and the boys just told us to hush and pushed us in the direction of the door.

This was not a penthouse. It was a block of high-rise flats in the middle of some rundown estate. Imagine the place Del Boy lived in *Only Fools and Horses*, well, it was worse than that. When we walked into their apartment, it was like a smack den. The curtains were all ripped, the walls were stained and the furniture was old and falling to pieces. It was horrendous and as I sobered up, I realised the situation was becoming more dangerous by the second. Lindsay headed straight for the bathroom because she was feeling sick – she had drunk far too much vodka and was about to see it in reverse.

We were all huddled in the hallway, not knowing what to do. There were guys in there who hadn't even been out that night, sitting in the living room smoking spliffs and drinking cans of lager. The place reeked.

The ringleader of the group – a black guy called Jerome – said to the guys who had been sitting in the flat, 'I told you I'd bring some birds back.'

When I heard that, I knew we had to get out of there. This was not going to be the fun party we all thought it would be.

Then another guy swung open a bedroom door, licked his lips and stood before us, stroking his cock, saying, 'Who's going to fuck me first?'

'What the hell!' I said in disgust, 'no one is having sex with you.'

'Why not? Why you think we brought you here?' he said, snarling in my direction.

When he carried on asking us over and over again and increasingly more forcibly, 'Which bitch is gonna get fucked first?' I started to panic. Honestly, I thought we would be raped in this God-awful crack place and no one would hear our cries for help.

When I peered into the kitchen there must have been another five black guys in there, all discussing which one of us they wanted to bang. After we heard them talking, we quickly bolted for the door, went down in the lift and attempted to get the hell out. But two of the guys had taken a separate lift down and when we got out at the bottom, they were there, waiting for us.

'Bitch, where you think you're going?' one guy asked me. 'You ain't leavin us!'

I have never been so terrified in all my life. I thought they were going to stab us and I felt such a fool for getting myself into this situation in the first place.

'We need to get back, we are leaving,' I replied.

'You just gonna fucking walk off? You gonna fucking diss me like that? You gonna embarrass me in front of my mates, you little slag!' he screamed in his Cockney accent.

'Yes, we are leaving. Now fuck off!' I shouted.

'Well, you ain't gonna get very far without your pal! She's upstairs, getting banged by my boy now.'

FUCK! In our haste we had forgotten all about Lindsay in the bathroom.

'Oh, Jesus!' I screamed. 'We need to get her out.'

I bolted back into the lift and made the girls come with me.

When the lads saw we had walked back in, they were all whooping and cheering. I pushed past three of them and banged loudly on the bathroom door.

'Lindsay, open the fucking door right now!' I screamed. I couldn't really hear anything apart from her groaning. 'Open the door now, Lindsay! We need to leave!'

Finally, she opened the door. She looked like a swan with a broken neck. We picked her up, carried her out, and ran as fast as we could away from that terrible place. After five minutes we flagged a black cab, which took us safely away and back to the car.

Looking back on that night we can all laugh about it now, but at the time it was one of the scariest moments of my life. Just a word of warning: don't ever go back to a party with people you don't know. Guys like that do not want to be your friend, ladies. All those fellas wanted was a suck or a fuck, and because they had basically paid for our night, they thought they were entitled to it. You can't fight someone off when you're in a vulnerable position after drinking alcohol. Don't make stupid errors of judgement. There's a world out there full of opportunists, so be safe, be wise and be careful!

Chapter Fourteen
FAME CALLING

People always ask me just how I wound up on *The Valleys*. Sometimes they genuinely want to know my story, and others – well, they want tips on how to bag themselves a role on TV. So if you're one of the ones who want to know what producers and media bods are looking for, listen up!

But first, a word of warning: think carefully before you sign your life away. Being on a reality TV show is all about being exposed. And that exposure includes everyone from your family, friends, neighbours and schoolteachers to your old flames, even your uncle's dog. People who used to know you will talk shit about you, and if you're unconcerned about the real likelihood that your laundry will be aired, your worst moments shown in detailed focus and your ability to go wild there for all the world to see, then I suppose you'll be fine. On the other hand, if you value your privacy and reputation intensely, reality TV stardom may not be for you so give it up before the going gets tough.

I'd always dreamed of being on TV, being a singer or a famous model, but I never did anything proactive about it. My mum never pushed me in that direction and besides, she could never have afforded for me to go to fun classes in the evening.

I'd never even heard of how you would go about getting on a reality show. For me, it all happened by chance. I was taking my little brother Regan into town for a haircut to a place called Ozy's salon in June 2012. The lady who owned it, Jodie, said some people had just been in, looking for youngsters to audition for a Welsh reality TV show. She told me she had passed on Harrison's and my number because we were both crazy party animals. At first I didn't think anything of it, but it sounded exciting. I asked Jodie what number she gave them because I used to lose my mobiles all the time then and I would forever be getting new SIM cards. The number she read out was wrong, and I'd be lying if I said I wasn't slightly miffed, because I thought the opportunity sounded fun.

Luckily, she did have a leaflet. It was black, with bright pink lettering on the front. The pamphlet simply said: 'ARE YOU THE NEXT WELSH REALITY TV STAR? CONTACT US NOW IF YOU'RE FUNNY, WILD, OUTRAGEOUS, SEXY AND OUTGOING'. I stood there, looking at the leaflet in my hand, and debated whether or not to call the number. Everyone in the salon was egging me on to call but I got nervous doing it in front of them, so I slid the leaflet into my bag and as usual, forgot all about it.

One day, I was having a particularly bad day sat in front of the computer screen at the energy company, going out of my mind. I remember feeling so fed up and miserable. I wanted to lie down, so I put my arms and head on the desk. I just wanted to give up and resign, but I couldn't because I desperately needed the money. As I peered towards my bag on the floor, I saw the black and pink leaflet inside like a flashing beacon, calling me to pick it up. It must have been a week since I'd first been handed it in the hair salon. There was literally nothing to lose, so I walked to the bathroom and dialled the number. My heart was in my mouth as I heard the ringtone buzzing on the other end.

'Hello?' said a girl's voice.

'Um, hi, um, I saw your leaflet about the show and um...' I didn't really know what to say. I hadn't prepared myself for any of what she was about to ask, '...and well, I thought I'd give you a call.'

'OK,' said the girl, 'And your name is...?'

'Lateysha Grace.'

'And what makes you think you would be good on a reality show, Lateysha?'

'Well, um, I dunno really, people are always telling me I'm pretty crazy and a good laugh.'

'Pretty and crazy, and a good laugh,' she repeated those words back to me as if she was noting everything down. 'So, you think you're pretty, Lateysha?'

I knew she had misheard me, but I just went along with her line of questioning. I also started to relax a little and just answered as honestly as I possibly could.

'Yeah, I do. I'm fucking stunning!' I laughed. 'I get loads of attention from boys. I always pull them even though I have a boyfriend.'

'Oh, my word, so you don't mind cheating on your boyfriend? Does he know?' she asked with enthusiasm.

'No, of course not and what he doesn't know, doesn't hurt him,' I said, shrugging my shoulders.

I knew I had this girl's interest, she was laughing along with me.

'So, tell me what you like to do at the weekends, Lateysha?'

'Well, I go out all the time with my friends. I love getting dressed up, going out, getting drunk and partying.'

'Ha, ha! So, I take it you're over eighteen then?'

'Yeah, I'm eighteen… just. But I've been drinking for years. I'm a bit of a wild child,' I sniggered.

When I think back now, everything I said must have been music to her ears because she invited me to come and meet the team a few days later.

'You sound great, Lateysha. Can I give you an email address so you can forward some photos of yourself? And then can you come to Cardiff for an audition?'

'Yeah, hang on, I'll just get a pen,' I said, as I rummaged round in my bag for an eyeliner and the back of a receipt. Using my kohl pencil, I scribbled down the email as clearly as I could.

'OK, Lateysha, well, it was good to talk to you. We'll be in touch,' she said, and she hung up.

Exhilarated, I walked back to my desk. I had a good feeling about the way the phone call had gone and I hoped they would like the look of me. I mean, come on, how could they not?

I scanned through all my Facebook pictures, trying to find the most glamorous and sexy ones. In the end I sent four of the most disgraceful, wild, ass-baring snaps I could find. In them, I was either draped all over a guy, swigging from a vodka bottle, or parading my body round in some way. They must have liked them because literally ten minutes after I sent the photos they were sending me details of where to meet.

Unfortunately they wanted me to meet them the next day in Cardiff. I didn't have the day off work and I had literally only £20 to my name, which would just about cover the cost of the petrol for the trip.

I was upfront with my boss and told her I needed the day off to attend an audition for a reality show. She was great about it and told me to go for it.

My friend Harrison and me had both been given an interview. I drove my blue Mini up to the Sleeperz Hotel in Cardiff and sat waiting for about an hour. All the time I kept seeing other young hopefuls leave with huge smiles on their faces. I looked over at Harrison, who was nervously biting his nails before a researcher called his name. As he walked off, I wished him good luck and now all I could do was wait. When he came back half an hour later, he too was grinning broadly.

'I smashed that, 'Teysha,' he told me.

'*Really*? What did they ask you? What did you have to do?' I said.

'They asked me what I did for a living so I told them I wash pets' bums,' he said, laughing to himself. He wasn't lying either – at that time he was working for a pet groomer.

Before he could tell me much else, it was my turn to wow the producers. When they called my name, I stood up confidently and wiggled down the short black dress I was wearing. I chose it because it showed off my ample curves and teamed it with a huge gold statement necklace, a leopard fur coat, super-high heels and the brightest pillar-box red lip gloss you could imagine. I'd got up extra early to contour my face make-up, blend my eye shadow and fit fake eyelashes. My hair was a deep brown colour, which I'd curled with tongs and I sassily tossed it over my shoulders as I walked over to the interview room.

'Come in, Lateysha, take a seat,' said the lady, pointing to a chair in front of a white backdrop.

There was one camera pointing to where I was sitting and three other faceless, nameless people sat behind a desk, making notes and whispering to each other. I sat down and shrugged off my coat, giving them an eyeful of my heaving bust.

'So, Lateysha, can you introduce yourself to the camera,

please, and tell us what you do in an upbeat, friendly manner,' a man said.

Instantly, I became nervous, but I supposed that was what I was there for – time to turn on the charm!

Clearing my throat, I said in the most enthusiastic manner I could, while grinning broadly, 'Hey, I'm Lateysha Grace and I work in a dead-end admin job all the hours God sends for absolute peanuts! I spend all the money I earn on making myself look stunning so I can bag a rich boyfriend. Either that, or I'm gonna be famous!'

The team laughed and I knew at once I'd broken the ice.

'Take it you wouldn't mind if you had to leave your job to be on the show, then?' one asked, giggling.

'Absolutely not! I was born to be on TV, I've always wanted to be in the limelight,' I said.

'So, what would be your dream job?' he continued.

'I would love to be an actress, or a model or a singer. That's always been my dream,' I replied.

'So, tell us about your typical night out...'

'OK, so I would spend about three hours getting ready and I won't leave until I know I look stunning. I go round to my friend's house and there, we'll get pissed on vodka before we head into town. Everyone knows me in Port Talbot and when I'm smashed, I request Beyoncé and dance crazy all night! Even when I'm walking down the street, people call me Beyoncé!'

They began to laugh at my unabashed arrogance.

'Do you think you look like Beyoncé?' one of them asked.

'Yeah, don't you? She's lush!'

'And what about boys?' one of them asked. 'Do you do well with the fellas?'

'Oh, yeah, I always pull boys.'

'But it says here, you have a boyfriend?' another said, peering down at his notes.

'Yeah, that's right. I've been with him for five years. I know it's wrong to cheat on him but sometimes I just can't help myself.'

'Do you not feel guilty?' he asked.

'I do, but when you have a footballer giving you attention it's hard to say no,' I smirked.

'*Footballer?*' his eyes perked up. 'Anyone we would know?'

I named quite a few of the Swansea squad and they just sat there, looking stunned.

'So, you want to be a WAG?' asked the lady.

'Yeah, why not? Have you seen their lifestyle, clothes and cars? I would love to be a WAG and have no money worries.'

I carried on chatting myself up, making myself sound like an easy girl and a drunken idiot with all my stories, but after about twenty minutes they felt they'd got enough material.

'Well, Lateysha,' one of the guys said, shaking his head. 'You certainly are a character. We've enjoyed talking to you. We'll be in touch, I'm sure.'

'Thanks,' I smiled. 'Nice to meet you all.'

I picked up my fur jacket, slung it over my shoulder and strutted out of there, already knowing I'd nailed it. I know this sounds big-headed but I could tell immediately by the way the panel had reacted, they loved me. You know when you just know? Well, I knew then there was a good chance I would never have to work at the energy company again. And I was fucking delighted!

About a week later, I got another call to go back to Cardiff to meet the big producers Manus Wynne and Fiona O'Sullivan of True North, the production company who made *The Valleys*, along with Steve Regan, one of the heads of MTV.

This time I wore black leggings, a Versace tracksuit jacket, a small vest top (again, cut pretty low) and some skyscraper ankle boots. I had instructions to meet them in a café called Mocha Lounge and when I showed up, it was clear all three were pleased to see me. They'd heard all about the Beyoncé wannabe. This time, the conversation was a lot less formal. There were no cameras; it was just a lengthy in-depth chat over a coffee.

The chat I had with them was weird, though, for it became more of a heart-to-heart than an interview. It was almost as if they had slipped truth serum in my water. I began divulging everything about my life – too much, if I'm honest.

I'd just started seeing another guy behind my boyfriend Ryan's back and I remember telling them about the whole affair. I don't know why, but they had this unique way of getting information out of me with very little persuasion. On some level I must have wanted to tell them, I suppose, to show just how daring and unscrupulous I could be. I told them things I hadn't even told my best friends.

On the third meeting, I wore an orange body-con and this time I took Ryan with me. They hadn't requested to see him; I just didn't want to go on my own. I have to say he was so supportive throughout the whole process. Personally, I don't know many boyfriends who would have been encouraging their girlfriends to go and pursue their dreams. And all I could keep thinking was, this is my escape from you. I know I sound like a bitch for saying that, but like I've said before, I didn't have the guts to leave him. We'd been together so long we were just in a routine. We weren't happy – we argued all the time, we were cheating on each other – and it was no kind of true meaningful relationship. I know two-timing is never the answer, but I wanted to make myself feel better at the time. Those of you who have been in the same situation as me will be able to understand, I'm sure. If you have only ever had a lovely, faithful boyfriend in your life, then lucky you, but try not to judge me if you have never been in my shoes. I'm not saying it's right what I did, I'm just telling you what happened.

I turned up at the meeting spot, another small boutique café in Cardiff. As I looked round the room, I couldn't see any of the crewmembers anywhere. I asked the manager behind the bar and he knew nothing about the meeting. By now, I was feeling sick because my phone battery had gone, so no one could call me. All these thoughts flooded through my mind: had I got the wrong address, or maybe the wrong time or the wrong day? Pissed off and panicked, I paced up and down, looking out of the window every thirty seconds, but I still couldn't see anyone. Eventually, after about an hour, the producers and staff burst through the door.

'Sorry we're late,' said a young girl.

'I've been here an hour, where have you been?' I asked, like a diva.

'We had other people to see, Lateysha. There's a lot of waiting around in this line of work, get used to it!' she said, very abrasively.

I didn't say anything, but they left me waiting another hour while they had some sort of discussion. When they finally called me over, I couldn't hide my irritation.

'Fuck's sake, what have you been doing? Why have you been making me wait so long?' I demanded.

'Ha, ha!' Steve laughed. 'I fucking love this girl! She just says how it is.'

I knew then after Steve – who as I already mentioned is one of the heads of MTV – said that, I was a dead cert. He loved my forthright attitude.

'What's your type, Lateysha?' they asked.

'What do you mean, type?'

'You know, in a guy. What do you look for?'

'I haven't really got a type – I just like cool, unusual-looking guys, although they have to be tall and I love tattoos. Mixed race or white, it doesn't matter.'

'And say we put someone in the house like your ideal man. Would you get with him, despite having a boyfriend?'

'I don't know... I mean, it's not really stopped me in the past, so who knows?' I said with a smirk.

Steve threw his head back and laughed.

After I left the meeting that day, I walked off, knowing it was in the bag. I knew I had gained myself a place on the newest reality show about to hit the UK screens.

Sure enough, a week later I got the call from a producer to tell me I was a member of a show called *The Valleys* to be broadcast on MTV in the summer of 2012. The premise was to follow eight youngsters from the South Wales Valleys as we moved to Cardiff to bag our dream jobs with the help of two bosses.

I literally screamed the house down when I knew I'd been picked for the show. I mean, I'd been telling all my mates I was going on the show ever since my first interview, but at least now it was official. Everyone was delighted for me. My brother Regan was buzzing and so too were my friends. My friend Harrison, who had also had an interview, never progressed past round one, but still he was happy for me in my new adventure.

Ryan didn't really know what kind of show *The Valleys* was going to be, but I honestly thought it would make me a millionaire. I would say to him, 'Just wait and see, when I have all this money, I can build a proper future for us both', so he was happy for me fulfil my dream. Even then, in the back of my mind, I was actually planning my escape. If I made any money, it would be so I could finally be independent and not have to rely on a guy for anything.

My mum was also made up for me. She thought I was going into some kind of *Big Brother* programme. I don't think she realised I was signing up to the booze-fuelled, bed-hopping antics of *The Valleys*, so she gave me her blessing and told me to give it my best shot.

I can't tell you how deliriously happy I was to get a place on the show. I haven't had a good life, nothing has ever gone my way, but I thought maybe this was karma paying me back for all the bad shit I'd endured growing up. Finally, for once something was going my way. I would sit there daydreaming about getting into modelling, but I was hardly going to be discovered in the Valleys, was I? For me, moving to Cardiff was the only way forward and with the help of this new TV show, I was one step closer to my dream.

The only thing that could stop me now was my big secret – the court case – and I prayed no one would ever find out about it anytime soon.

Chapter Fifteen

TOUGH CHOICE

In between finding out I was a fully-fledged member of *The Valleys* and before we actually started filming, I had to deal with the most heart-breaking situation of my life. One of the most reckless things I've ever done, it was my own stupid fault and completely avoidable. I'm going to share it with you in the hope that you won't make the same mistake as me.

It was May 2012 when I made the tough decision to have an abortion.

First, let me give you a bit of background information. At the time I was still living with my then boyfriend Ryan in the house we shared in Skewen. By now, you'll know our relationship was a complete sham: zero love, zero affection or future together. We should have ended it, but five years is a long time with someone – you just can't throw it all away at once.

For me, the main problem was there was no trust. Ryan would go out for days on end, partying and getting pissed. He would switch his phone off and I would never be able to get hold of him.

127

What kind of boyfriend does that to his girlfriend? A shitty one!

At first, it would anger and upset me but after a while I just stopped caring – I suppose I stopped being in love. The rumours about him being a prolific cheat had been floating around for years, but nothing I could nail down as evidence. In my heart of hearts I knew what he was doing. You know the telltale signs. He was always hiding his phone. And when it wasn't hidden, it would be on silent and face down. It doesn't take a genius to work out he was up to no good, but I wasn't going to sit in the house waiting around for him all the time. If he was cheating on me, I could cheat on him, I decided.

I invited plenty of attention from guys. At the time I was texting loads of different people. I had necked on with a few, slept with a couple and also began a sexual relationship with a guy called Steven Caulker, who played for Swansea at the time but has since moved to Queens Park Rangers. He was tall, mixed race, good-looking and had that confident footie player swagger. We met on a night out in Swansea and I was instantly attracted to him. It was never going to be a real relationship or anything – I suppose the proper title for us would have been 'fuck buddies'.

Although I really liked him, I got the feeling he didn't like me as much as I did him. I know I couldn't trust Ryan, but I definitely couldn't have trusted a guy like Steven. You know what footie players are like! I suppose it was just instinct at first, but my worst fears were confirmed when one of my best friends called me and confessed she'd slept with him. I was raging and so upset with them both but her defence was, 'Well, you have Ryan, you can't get mad!' Er, yes, I could – that is still breaking the girl code, by the way.

I was going out all the time at this point, it was the only thing keeping me sane. Ryan didn't give a fuck about me, so I did as I pleased. One night I was out with my friend Kim in Revolution and I saw a guy called Antony. We had previous history – I'd slept with him two years before at Harrison's house when Ryan and me were taking a break.

When I saw him again after all this time, I had forgotten how nice-looking he was. He reminded me of Max from The Wanted – skinhead, blue eyes, muscly, with a cool sense of style. I really fancied the guy.

As soon as he saw me, he made a beeline in my direction. We did the usual chit-chat, he bought me a drink, we flirted and made suggestive advances. And then he invited me back to a house party. Of course Kim and I just wanted the night to carry on, so we went without question.

At the house party, Antony was all over me. It was clear what he wanted, right from the get-go. I was so tired of Ryan and his cheating that I didn't give him a second thought and not long after I'd arrived, Antony and me were full-on shagging. I'd like to tell you it was in some cosy, romantic setting, but come on, does that sound like me? We ended up fucking on the landing upstairs, while all the other partygoers carried on drinking downstairs. I suppose it was a bit of a thrill, really: knowing we could have been caught by anyone. It added to the excitement of the situation.

Let me tell you, I gave Antony the ride of his life that night. We did it every which way you can imagine. Him on top, me on top, doggy, reverse cowgirl, against the wall, on all fours... you name it, we did it. Everyone downstairs could hear us pounding away. Me moaning and groaning with pleasure, him breathing loudly as he banged me harder and harder. Who knows what they thought of us.

The worst thing about this little liaison was that because it had all happened so fast and we were so hot for each other, in the heat of the moment we never bothered to use a condom. I know, it was a stupid mistake and I'm 100 per cent advising against ever having sex without a condom, not just because of the risk of getting pregnant, but because of the risk of contracting an STD. Trust me, make sure you bag up, but as you will find out, I learnt the hard way.

It was while I was on all fours that Antony announced he'd come inside me. Quickly, I ran to the loo and tried to pee the excess out, hoping this would help matters. To be honest, I didn't give it much thought after that. I didn't promise myself to get the Morning After Pill or anything. I thought I'd risk it and everything would be all right. Big mistake. HUGE!

When I came out of the bathroom, Antony got me a drink and we spent the rest of the party pretty much ignoring each other. Weird considering he'd just been inside me, but it's not like we wanted to be an item or anything, we were just satisfying our mutual needs. This might make me sound like a slag or whatever, but as far as I'm concerned, I enjoy sex and sometimes you just have to get your fill.

That night I stayed at Kim's and the next day she dropped me off home. In the cold light of day I felt awful. I'd had unprotected sex with a guy the night before and now I was going back home to chill with my boyfriend.

As soon as I walked in the door, he was suspicious. He kept asking me where I'd been the previous evening and who I'd been with. I could feel my face flushing as lie after lie left my lips.

The guilt was a horrible feeling and after that, I never wanted to have sex with Ryan again. To be totally honest, we hadn't had sex for months anyway, but now I never wanted him near me at all. I would make up all kinds of excuses not to do it with him or I would stay at my friends' houses so we couldn't spend time alone together. I know it was wrong, but come on, the guy had been treating me like shit for years and there was only so much I could take.

A few weeks later, I was checking my calendar in work and I still hadn't come on my period. I wasn't the most regular of girls, but I thought after I'd been with Antony there was a slight chance I might be pregnant. It definitely couldn't have been Ryan's because like I said, I hadn't been having sex with him.

I called my mother immediately and told her the situation. Unlike most mothers, who might have hit the roof, she was really cool and calm about the whole thing, which helped. She told me to buy myself a test and head for her house after work.

Those last few hours in work were the longest of my life. Time seemed to be standing still, but when I finally left, I hurried round to Mum's and took the test almost as soon as I got through the door. It only took a couple of minutes to confirm my worst fears.

I was pregnant.

I couldn't believe it and worst of all, I didn't know whose baby it was. It could have been Steven's, or it might have been conceived after that mad night of passion with Antony.

My mum kept saying to me, ''Teesh, you have to tell Ryan.'

'No way! Are you crazy? I'm not telling him,' I said.

'You can't just get rid of his baby without telling him,' she implored me.

'Erm, Mum, there's a good chance it's *not* his baby.'

'*What?*'

'I've been seeing a couple of other guys,' I said sheepishly.

My mum closed her eyes and shook her head. She had me at the same age as I was then and she wasn't at all happy that I seemed to be in the same situation. She didn't want me to be a single parent as she herself had been, especially if I wasn't in a relationship with the dad.

'When did you sleep with them?' she asked, still astonished at my confession.

'All within four days of each other, so I can't be sure who the dad is,' I admitted, shame-faced.

Mum wanted to do the right thing and call up these lads but there was no way I was going to let that happen. I didn't know what to do – I was due to go into *The Valleys* in two weeks' time, I had a court case looming and I was pregnant by one of two potential men. Now my life was like an episode of *Jeremy Kyle*.

I've always been a big believer in pro-choice and a woman's right to make a decision about her own body, but when I was put in that situation myself it was the hardest choice of my life. In the end I chose to terminate the pregnancy, but believe me when I say that I, rightly, agonised over it.

Many people will disagree with me. You can debate with me all you want when it comes to the arguments for anti-abortion and the sanctity of life. Trust me, I wasn't flippant in my decision, I thought about it long and hard. I spoke to my friends, family, and did lots of research into the procedure. If you ever find yourself in the same situation, which I hope you don't, make sure you know everything before making your mind up. Terminating a foetus is a decision that should never be taken lightly. I don't see it as a method of birth control, and back then I didn't either – I was just a very stupid girl.

My reasons were selfish, I admit. I had just been given a place on *The Valleys* – something I had wanted for years. This was my breakout of Port Talbot and into a career that could really set me up for life. Having said that, even if I didn't have the show coming up I would still have decided on a termination because what life would the baby have had? I couldn't afford to look after a child. Also, I was pretty sure whoever the father was – Steven or Antony – they weren't going to support it and I am not one of those people willing to live off the state. I myself had nothing growing up and if I was to have a baby, I would want to be financially secure and able to give it everything it could possibly need. I would want to be in circumstances where I could provide for my child, no matter what. There are sixteen-year-old girls in my town who have had babies and kept them. I always look at them and think what kind of a life is that for a young girl?

The following day I made an appointment with my doctor and after giving me the biggest dressing down of my life about unsafe sex, he gave me more bad news: the NHS wouldn't be able to fit me in for the abortion for another three weeks.

Three weeks was far too late because I would have started filming for *The Valleys*. Already, I would be in the house. The doctor looked at me in disgust when I told him my situation and he was completely unhelpful and unsympathetic. He suggested I go into the house, leave one day, have an abortion and go back in. Was he serious? Did he know what show I was going in for? In the end, my only other option was to go to a private clinic called Marie Stopes.

When I called the clinic and explained my situation they said they could fit me in the following week, but that that luxury would come with a price tag of £500. At this point I had no money. Nothing, zero to my name. I couldn't ask Ryan for any cash without arousing suspicion and my mum didn't have any, either.

The only thing to do was bite the bullet and text the lad I thought was the dad. I knew Steven would have the money, he was a footie player and never short of cash, but I had this overriding feeling it was Antony's, so I messaged him. I could quite easily have made Steven pay, but I wasn't willing to drop that on him if deep down I knew he probably wasn't the dad. Typing out a text to Antony, I said, 'We need to talk. I'm pregnant.'

Being the lovely supportive guy he was, he replied saying, 'Fuck off, how do you know it's mine?'

'I've worked out the dates and it is yours!' I typed back in anger.

'What are you going to do? We can't keep it Tesha,' he texted back.

'I know, I'm not going to, but I just thought you should know.' I was completely pissed off with him; he really didn't care.

'I need some money for the abortion, it's £500,' I told him.

Antony replied, telling me he had no money because – get this – he was going to Malia with his mates! I was raging when he told me that. Man enough to plant his seed inside me, he should be man enough to deal with the situation. As far as I was concerned, he was taking no responsibility for his actions. I was fuming!

Later that day he called me and somehow managed to sweet talk me round on the phone, explaining that if I paid for the abortion, he would pay me back when he got back from holiday. Stupidly, I believed him and so I spent the next four hours securing a loan from a short-term lender, Moneypig, for the full amount.

The initial meeting with a nurse was fine because my mum came with me. At this point I started to detach myself from the pregnancy and everything seemed like a bad dream but I'll admit to being nervous, waiting in that room, because I had no clue what to expect. You can read all the information you want to on the Internet to make yourself as prepared as possible but actually going through the situation is still very nerve-wracking.

They gave me an ultrasound to see how far gone I was and then they told me I was six weeks. I remember my mum working out the date when it would have been born. 'Ah, it would have been a December baby,' she said, much to my annoyance. I didn't need reminders like that – I didn't want to think of this thing growing inside me as a real person. The nurse talked to me again to make sure I was fully aware of what I was doing. I agreed it was the right decision for me at the time and so she gave me a pill to swallow, which would destroy the life inside me.

It seemed almost too easy.

Two days later, I had to return to the clinic to have another pill inserted in me. For this appointment Antony (the likely dad) and my best friend Harrison came with me for moral support. The nurse gave me another ultrasound and told me to open my legs while she inserted the pill inside me. I felt so sick, not only because of the drugs but because I had just ended a life. If the circumstances had been different (like, if it had been Ryan's baby), then who knows, I probably would have kept it, despite the show. Deep down, even though we had cheated on each other many times, I still loved Ryan in a way. He was my first love and you never quite lose that affection for someone. Maybe it could have been a fresh start for us, I'll never know.

After it was over, I went back to Harrison's house that evening and Antony came with us. I think he wanted to look like he was doing the right thing; he didn't want to get off straight after the procedure. When he was in Harrison's house he was so uncomfortable, he didn't know what to do because I couldn't stop crying. I'd never felt so emotional, it must have been the hormones because I was literally balling my eyes out.

Antony tried to lighten the mood and was asking me all about *The Valleys*. The show had been the talk of the town for a while and it was rumoured his ex-girlfriend, Nicole Morris, was going in the house too. I knew of Nicole, but because of Antony, we didn't get on. We would see each other on nights out and always make snarl faces. I remember saying to him, 'I hope she's not in the house, it's going to be awkward now I've just aborted your baby.' Antony kind of shrugged and laughed. He was nervous of any mention of the procedure and after about ten minutes, he left, telling me he would pay me back the money after his holiday.

I don't want to go into the nitty-gritty of what happened, but I hope that revealing this kind of detail will deter any young girl from getting into the same situation as me. Over the next six hours, I was in a terrible way. My stomach was in knots, like terrible period pains, and there was more blood than I ever thought. I went to the toilet and then I saw it: a little lump of cells that would have become my child, had I let it continue to grow inside me. Completely freaked out, I shouted for Harrison. He came into the bathroom and told me I had to put it out of my mind. I felt awful, flushing the chain and letting it go down the pan. In the end he had to do it for me because I just couldn't face it.

After that I watched every chick flick Harrison had and we consumed a year's worth of chocolate in one night. My head was a complete mess: I was so screwed, I couldn't face Ryan, so I told him I was staying at Harrison's for the night. To this day, he has no idea what I went through, but now I suppose he will if he ever reads this book. Although he probably won't be surprised.

Honestly, the abortion isn't the worst part; it's the thoughts that follow it. Sometimes I wonder what my life would have been like if I'd had my baby, but at the same time I know I did what was right for me and I'm OK with that.

When Antony got back from Malia, I asked him if he had the money to pay me back – I wanted him to at least pay half. That's the least he could have done, I thought. Although I texted and

Facebooked him constantly, he ignored me. I think it's gutless when a guy leaves it all up to the girl to sort out what ought to have been a joint problem. I should have known Antony would renege on our agreement. Still, the procedure was over and I had to look forward to my new adventure on *The Valleys*. I couldn't worry about it anymore.

I've always said I've never had any regrets in life, and I thought I didn't until I started writing this book. The whole episode with the abortion could have been avoided so easily, and I will always regret going through that experience. It's not big or clever and doesn't make you grown up. In fact having that kind of careless attitude towards sex makes you really immature. I regret the way I treated Ryan, too; maybe that makes me sound stupid because he wasn't exactly a gentleman to me but two wrongs don't make a right. I know he will agree that we should have split way sooner than we did but neither of us had the guts. But let's get one thing straight, we were both as bad as each other. It's not an excuse and I don't want him to take all the flack for the downfall of our relationship because we both disrespected each other. I'm not saying it's right, that's just the way it was. I'm learning from my mistakes every day and I'm telling you about them too so you don't make the same ones. Being in an unhappy relationship is tough, but you only get one shot at this life, so make your days count and when things are no longer making you smile, it's time to move on.

Chapter Sixteen

A NEW BEGINNING

It was the end of May 2012, when we were due to join the house. About a week prior to our first filming day, a researcher called to tell me what to pack. I still had no idea what to expect from the TV show, but I was so ready for whatever they were about to throw at me. Bring it on, I thought.

The girl on the phone buttered me up something chronic and filled my head with all sorts of flattery. She told me they absolutely loved me exactly the way I was and not to change anything about myself, appearance-wise. This included dyeing my hair. They wanted me to keep it blonde with my horrible dark-black roots. Oh, the shame! I can't believe I let them talk me into keeping my hair like that, I really didn't like it but I did what needed to be done.

Next, I was specifically told they wanted me to wear a gold dress. Apparently, I was pegged to be this Beyoncé/Lil' Kim character. I didn't have much money, so I searched eBay for something suitable and eventually won a one-shoulder bandage number to wear for my debut. But I did splash out on some new gold, silver and black Johnrey Campbell heels. Super-high, with a clunky wooden sole, they were an eye-watering £130, but I didn't care – I had to have them for my entrance.

I had instructions to go to a hotel in Cardiff and stay the night there. The next day, I would be taken off to the house for my first day's filming. I didn't want to go on my own, so I got Ryan to come with me. He was supportive and worried for me, I could tell. That last night with him was nice. We spent the night cwtching and kissing, it was like we had just met all over again. I don't know why we were so close that night; I think maybe because we both knew it was over from then on. I was going on this mad adventure and we both understood I wouldn't be the same person when it was finished. I was going to be this massive celebrity – at least that's what I thought at the time.

When the next morning came around, I said my goodbyes to Ryan and he left me to get ready. I was a mixture of nerves and excitement. I had no idea what I was letting myself in for, but I couldn't think about that now; I had to transform myself into Lateysha the Diva, like the crew had specifically requested.

I started with my make-up, which I slapped on like there was no tomorrow. I'd heard people say you have to apply loads more make-up for TV, so I really went to town. I wore thick heavy eyeliner, long, lush lashes and my favourite pillar-box red lipstick for that all-important pout. My hair took the longest to style. I'd borrowed my friend's large crimper to do it. Honestly, that morning I thought I looked stunning, but when I look back now at the first episode I'm like, 'Wow, I was hanging!'

At around 10am, I got a phone call from a crewmember, who took me to an apartment not far from the studio. I say 'studio' because even though it was meant to be a house, it wasn't, and that's what I used to forget at times. To put it bluntly, the house was a TV set we lived on, slept on, ate on and shat on.

In the crew apartment, I waited patiently while they searched my bags. They were looking for any contraband that would give me access to the outside world. Phones, cameras and iPads, etc. were strictly forbidden. Also, we weren't allowed to take anything in, like books or magazines, nothing that could distract us from the action.

It's probably a good idea to know everything about a show before you are due to star in it, but I'll admit I didn't do my homework. We were each given a DVD of *Geordie Shore* so we could watch episodes and see how the show was filmed, edited and so on, but I never got round to actually viewing any of the programmes. At that time I must have been one of the only people in the UK who hadn't seen an episode of *Geordie Shore*. Don't get me wrong, now I watch it because I'm friendly with the cast, but back then I was going into this experience blind.

After the crew were satisfied I wasn't smuggling anything in my case, they were ready to start. I was instructed to drive my car round the house while a cameraman got in the car to film my arrival.

'Loads of energy, Lateysha! Tell us how excited you are to be here. Don't forget, you are a diva!' said the producer, giving me directions.

When I pulled up outside the house, it was nothing like I was expecting.

For starters, it was on a main high street, sandwiched between an estate agent's office and a Jamaican restaurant, which I thought was crazy. Shouldn't we be on the outskirts of town so we could make as much noise as we wanted? I'm sure the neighbouring businesses weren't happy.

Then another crewmember handed me the key to the front

door and when I opened it, I half-expected to be welcomed by a gang of new young people, but I was actually the first one to arrive. I'd been told to play up my larger-than-life character and be as excited as possible about the new house, so that's exactly what I did. I squealed with delight as I looked around the house for the first time. And to be fair, it was absolutely amazing! All the rooms were bright, funky and modern. It looked like a show home that had leapt straight out of the pages of a magazine. The only difference was all the camera equipment strategically placed around the house. As soon as I saw it all, it made me instantly apprehensive. Like I said before, I was forgetting I wasn't in a house; I was living on a TV set and my every move would now be filmed, captured, recorded and scrutinised by anyone who watched. Then again, this is what I signed up for. It was such a surreal experience.

The pressure of being the first one through the door is you have to try and be entertaining while having no one else to interact with. I'm pretty sure that's why they chose to send me in first because I was quite possibly the most brazen loudmouth of the bunch. I remember running around like an idiot, checking out all the rooms, and screaming, 'This is a diva house!', but this was only because I'd been told to play up my fabricated diva-esque image.

It wasn't long before another housemate arrived. In walked this handsome, buff, living, talking Ken doll called Aron, wearing a T-shirt cut so low you could see his tits. What was it with those tops? Within minutes of meeting me for the first time, Aron shimmied down his jeans and started showing me his kickboxing moves! I was impressed, not by his moves but by the bulge in his boxers. My word, the lad looked like he had a huge piece on him!

Next to arrive was Chidgey, who wasn't my type at all. He

looked like he loved himself and I don't go for guys like that. If I get with a guy, they should feel lucky to have me, but with Chidgey, I got the feeling it would be the other way around: a guy who would nail and bail.

Then in walked someone I was more than interested in: luscious Leeroy. As soon as I clapped eyes on him, I was smitten. He was exactly my type – mixed race, cool dresser, with a couple of tattoos and a confident attitude. When he started rapping, I could have pounced on him. *I could be Beyoncé to his Jay-Z*, I thought. I couldn't help but flirt with him from the offset.

Next to rock up was Jenna and I remember thinking, *Fuck! Now I have competition.* I couldn't take my eyes off her massive fake boobs, long, straight natural hair and her skinny body – and she was wearing a gold dress almost identical to my own. It couldn't have been a coincidence, I'm pretty sure the producers must have told her to buy a gold dress too, just to wind us both up. She also brought her yappy dog Princess, who would not stop barking at me. Honestly, it was doing my head in. I instantly pegged Jenna as the typical ditzy bimbo and that's a role she played up to, despite being a clever girl with a law degree.

When Nicole walked in, my heart sank. Like I said before, I'd never befriended her but I knew of her because I had history with her ex-boyfriend, Antony. I knew instantly there would be huge arguments between us, especially because after about two minutes of walking into the house, she revealed to everyone that I had a boyfriend. *Nice one, Nic*, I thought. This was a fact I'd wanted to discuss with the house myself, not have someone else blurt it out for me.

Leeroy was stunned because I'd been overtly flirting with him ever since he stepped over the threshold.

'Oh, my days! You have a boyfriend?' he asked, shocked.

'We're on a break,' I told him, which was a complete lie. 'Thanks, Nicole, for dropping that bombshell!'

From that moment on, I completely hated Nicole. The only reason she did it was because I had slept with her ex-boyfriend.

Next to waltz through the lime green doors was Liam. Now, I'm not going to lie: when I first saw him, I wondered why they cast him. There are so many good-looking boys around so why had they had chosen Liam? Unattractive and a bit goofy, totally average, I was pretty stunned they would have a guy like that in the mix. I knew hundreds of fit boys they could have had in his place. Casting him had been a huge disappointment.

The first thing he did after walking in was stand in Princess's dog shit and I could not stop laughing.

'Eurgh, you've stood in shit! You fucking stink!' I laughed, while Liam looked embarrassed. It wasn't a nice thing to do, I agree, but I was playing up to the cameras. Understandably, Liam and me didn't get off on the right foot and we clashed pretty much every day throughout the five weeks we lived together.

The only other housemate I hated in equal measure was Carley. She staggered in, looking dishevelled, in a revealing midi dress. And she had been in the house about thirty seconds before she decided to whip her tits out. I mean, really? Couldn't she have waited until she got to know everyone's names first? I looked at her in disgust, thinking, *Oh my God, what a slut*! I'm not daft, though, I know the producers probably told her to go in there and act like a complete trollop, but at the time I just thought she had no self-respect.

Later that night, we all went out to Cardiff's hottest club, Glam. My opinion of Carley didn't change there, either – in fact, it only got worse. She ended up getting completely smashed and started dancing like an absolute slag in the club. All night I was giving her evils. I couldn't believe the way she was carrying on. I mean, I was all up for a bit of sexy dancing, but she was just a complete train wreck. It was like watching an animal that had escaped captivity.

Weirdly, our shared hatred of Carley that night brought Nicole and me together. I remember standing beside her, just staring at Carley and her antics. We began chatting and slagging her off and I suppose it broke the ice. After that our relationship changed; I remember thinking Nicole was such a nice girl and I didn't even know why I hated her in the first place.

The more pissed I got, the flirtier Leeroy became and soon we ended up necking in the club. The fact I had a boyfriend didn't even cross my mind. I was like a new girl and I completely forgot about my own life back in Port Talbot, with Ryan. In hindsight I was being a complete bitch. I often wondered why I hadn't just ended things with Ryan before I entered the house, but then how would that have looked? 'Ryan, thanks for the last five years but I'm dumping you now to go on a reality TV show.' I would still have looked like a bitch for doing that. I couldn't win. Still, I know right from wrong and it's really wrong to cheat on someone, especially when they were probably going to watch it on TV. That's not just wrong, that's humiliating someone and it's not me. I'm not a bully or a nasty person. I don't want people to get that impression of me. I was being self-centred. I got carried away and if I could turn back the clock, I would have finished with Ryan properly. The last thing I wanted to do was hurt him anymore.

When we arrived back at the house, Leeroy carried on flirting with me. He took me in the shower, obviously thinking he was going to bang me, and then showed me down to the basement bedroom, away from everyone else. As if... He wasn't about to get a grip of my sweet ass without putting a serious shift in first.

In the end we settled for a cwtch. After all, I had plenty of time to get with him.

That night I went to bed and fighting my drunken stupor, tried to reflect on the day's events. It had been a crazy experience and I wasn't sure what I was letting myself in for. I was now living in a house with a wild bunch of sexed-up reprobates and if the first twenty-four hours were anything to go by, this would be one hell of a rollercoaster ride.

Chapter Seventeen

VALLEY LIFE

I settled into Valley life pretty quickly. Obviously, we weren't all there just to get pissed, argue and shag each other. We were actually attempting to start new careers for ourselves. Like I said before, I was trying to become a model and my first photo shoot involved absolutely no glitz and glam. I was in a tiny bikini, on a freezing cold beach, while catty Nicole decided to make use of her sea-life props. I had crabs and fish all over me! It's funny to watch back now, but at the time I was beyond raging, although the most hilarious part of that day was seeing Chidgey trying to pull his moody blue steel pose with a stinking dead octopus on his head. I was crying with laughter and the more we all laughed, the angrier and more self-conscious he became. It still cracks me up when I think back to it now; it was hysterical! All the cast and crew were rolling around, laughing – Chidgey must have felt like an absolute knob.

The house dynamics were good up until Natalee, Chidgey's ex, turned up. Obviously the producers threw her into the mix to cause trouble between the alpha male and the rest of the females. And it worked, because no sooner had she walked in the front door than Chidgey became like a cowering dog, hiding from her. I'll admit at first we'd all heard about his ex being a bit of a psycho slag, so when she arrived I hoped she wouldn't try and make herself top girl in the house because that role belonged to me.

She did come across as quite bitchy and confrontational but now I know Natalee, I suspect this was just because she was nervous. But the friction between Nicole and I disappeared pretty quickly, despite the producers wanting us to be arch-enemies. We just couldn't be horrid to each other and I'm glad those feelings of hatred vanished virtually straight away. In fact, we got on so well, we became like a pair of lesbians – and believe me, we had not been told to do any of that.

As soon as we had a couple of drinks down our necks we became so flirty with each other. One minute we would be passionately snogging, the next pulling each other's dresses down and feeling each other up. I don't know what got into us; we must have been so sexually frustrated. I'm not gay or anything, but smooching with a girl is no different than with a boy. As far as I'm concerned, the mouth is gender-neutral and when I've had a few vodkas, I get the taste for lips. Of course I wasn't just kissing Nicole; it was any boy I liked the look of. I would stride up to the nearest hot guy, grab him round the back of the neck, pull him close to me and kiss his face off!

Speaking of being gay, Liam had come out to us on the show. I was glad he felt comfortable enough to tell us. I ran over to him and gave him a hug. Many of my friends back home had a hard time coming out as gay and I understood it is sometimes a difficult subject to talk about, especially in front of strangers. Liam might have thought I pitied him, I suppose, which wasn't the case; I just wanted to show him a little support. He said the way I behaved around him had changed since he had come out and commented I 'was all over him.' He said when I gave him a hug it had made him look like a dickhead. I apologised at the time saying I didn't mean to cause offence and then explained two of my best friends are gay, so I kind of knew what he must have been feeling like. But that's when Liam launched into a tirade saying 'you wouldn't have a fucking clue. You are thick as shit. You're a two-faced fucking idiot.' I couldn't believe it, the one time I was being genuinely caring, he had to throw it all back in my face, like I was doing it for some kind of attention. To me that says more about Liam than me, if he can construe something so innocent as something sinister.

As time went on all the girls began to bond, so much so that someone came up with the bright idea for us all to get matching tattoos. I say 'someone', well it was actually Jenna's idea, so yes, thank you Jen.

I was the first one of us to have a sheep scratched into my skin. I mean, what was going to happen when I had sex with a boy? How was I going to explain that?

While we were away from the house, we were told we were staying in Caerphilly for the evening. It was Carley's hometown and the producers had drafted in some decent-looking talent. I didn't know whether to believe them, though, because Valleys boys are generally below par, so I was pleasantly surprised and impressed when these four super-hunky Welsh wonders walked into the bar.

I felt like I hadn't had sex for a while; Nicole was the same. As we were both horny, we flirted outrageously with these men. We wanted them to know we were game straight from the off. It wasn't long before we were dragging these guys back to the house and preparing our foofs for the fellas, despite them still being sore from the tattoo.

Nicole and I decided we wanted a foursome. We were doing everything else together, so why not sex? But it had taken us so long to shower, shave, moisturise and put clean underwear on that we had begun to sober up. When the lads eventually climbed into bed with us and I felt them hard on me, I screamed. It occurred to me that these lads weren't all that and actually, they made me feel sick.

OK, I know we were the biggest cockteasers on the planet, but what could we do? Once our beer goggles were well and truly off, so were they! We told them the foursome wasn't going to happen and off they went, horny tails between their legs.

Later that night, another male got on my tits, but not in a good way. Leeroy, the one I once had the hots for, deliberately argued with me for no good reason. He started calling me names and saying I was hanging, trying to embarrass me in front of the whole group. If I was hanging, why did he try and get with me on the first night? It was because I'd rejected his advances and he couldn't get over the fact I had turned him down on that first night. I was never going to have sex with him in the house anyway, I still technically had a boyfriend and I'd promised my mum I wouldn't do that sort of thing for fear of embarrassing her. During the row I tried to laugh it off and give as good as I got, but deep down I was really hurt. Any girl would feel the same. I might come across as a tough cookie, but I'm big and strong enough to admit most of the time it's just a front.

Nicole, bless her, was the only one who stuck up for me against this pathetic attack; no one else was going to, because the majority of the house probably agreed with Leeroy. I remember Liam high-fiving Leeroy as he was having a go at me and it made me hate him even more. Seeing those two lads gang up on me was horrible and I didn't know how much more I could take. All the stress of those two dickheads, along with the other stresses I'd been through outside the Valleys, was finally taking its toll.

That night, I lay awake and my mind started to wander. Mainly, I was thinking about the abortion. If you've ever been through a termination then you'll know just how devastating it can be and I couldn't stop thinking about it. Add in the fact I was on a wild reality show, and had a secret court case hanging over my head, you can understand that I was pretty messed up when filming first started. Just one of those factors would make someone stressed, but I had to deal with it all at once. Sleep-deprived and hungover, I also felt hassled from arguing with the housemates and my hormones were all over the place, so I wasn't in a very good state of mind.

I remember for the first two weeks I was still wearing pads and tampons, which was awkward because all we ever did was get made to pose in skimpy underwear, but I managed to cover my tracks easily enough by telling everyone I was on my period. Every time I saw blood it was another reminder of the trauma I'd been through. It's difficult to put into words how I felt, but I'd feel a sharp stab of guilt for what I'd done and guilty for forgetting all about it and enjoying myself. Worst of all, the father had been Nicole's former boyfriend. She was now my closest friend in the house and I had to keep this secret to myself. I so badly wanted to share what I was going through, but I couldn't. Nicole was my only ally there, the one who had fought my corner against everyone. I feared she would hate me if I told her what was really going on and I couldn't take that risk.

As much as I didn't look like I was hurting on screen, I was. Deep down, I felt hollow. I was slapping on a brave face and trying to keep my spirits up when I was in the moment, but as soon as I had some downtime, sadness would take over me. Angry, confused and hurting, I was back to living the unhappy double-life I had tried so hard to escape from.

Chapter Eighteen

SECRET'S OUT

Every day while I was on *The Valleys*, I woke up worrying because the court date for the trial I was given had been set for 16 June 2012. The day was getting closer and still I hadn't told anyone at MTV or the production company. I'd panicked when I'd seen the date on the solicitor's letter because I knew I was going to be in the house when I was due to be in court.

Stupidly, I thought I would be able to wing it nearer the time and tell the crew I had to leave for a couple of days for a family emergency or some other made-up lie. The production company True North and MTV still knew nothing about the impending court action and I wasn't about to tell them.

Throughout my selection process they had asked me repeatedly if there was anything they needed to know and I had continually lied. I feared if they found out the truth, they would be tamping and most likely throw me off the show. No one could know. But like all secrets, they never stay that way forever and I was about to be found out in spectacular fashion.

One evening in the house they'd organised a farmers' fancy

dress party for us. All the lads were dressed as – you've guessed it – farmers, while the girls were kitted out in Little Bo Peep outfits. The costume was quite cute, actually; it was a pink gingham pinafore, knee-high white socks and a bonnet.

The night was in full swing, but I was feeling increasingly down about the rows in the house. When I looked around, everyone was having fun, but I didn't feel part of the group anymore. I couldn't handle the party and spent the majority of the night outside on my own.

After seeing how upset I was, the senior producer allowed me to call my mum. I needed to speak to someone who actually cared about me. As soon as I heard her familiar voice, I broke down in tears. I'd come to Cardiff to pursue my dream job of modelling and being on a new cool reality TV programme, but I had all this shit going on inside my head. The arguments with Liam and Leeroy had got to me more than anyone could know. I'm also a million per cent sure my emotions were still in turmoil after the secret abortion. I told my mum I was having second thoughts about being part of the programme and I wanted to leave. She was understanding and instead of saying something like, 'You've made your own bed, now you'll have to lie in it', she told me she would be waiting for me if I did want to go back to Port Talbot.

The only person I would be sad to leave was Nicole. It was crazy the way we had bonded in such a short space of time and I was genuinely heartbroken to be parting from her. I wished I could have told her about my abortion troubles, but as I've said before the fact that the baby was by her ex-boyfriend meant I didn't know how she would react. She had only just come into my life, I didn't want to upset her and make her hate me.

The producers agreed it would be OK if I left the house and saw my family for a few days. They could see how upset I was

154

and hoped if I had a break away, I would return to finish filming because they didn't want to lose me as part of the cast.

One of the more friendly producers, Natalie Grant, took me away from the house to the apartment the crew used for storing equipment so they could unhook my microphones and organise my travel home. I was always going to return to the show, but it was decided I should have a few days' break.

Meanwhile, back at the house I was about to be rumbled. You see, when we filmed party scenes on the show, the researchers drafted in 'extras' to party with and add some colour. One girl at the party just happened to be Paige Harris's best friend, Jade. As soon as I was gone she took great delight in telling everyone about how I'd assaulted her friend in a vicious nightclub attack. When the crew heard her story, they were, quite rightly, raging.

So there I was, sat in my little outfit, tears streaming down my face as I waited for a taxi to take me back to Port Talbot, blissfully unaware of the drama unfolding back at the house. It was only when the producer Natalie received a phone call from a crewmember who told her about Jade's revelation that I knew there was a problem. I could see Natalie's face drop when she was speaking on the phone and it didn't take a rocket scientist to figure out what she had just been told. I knew from then on, the jig was up.

Natalie sighed loudly and looked at me.

'Lateysha, Fiona, the head producer, is going to come over in a minute. She wants to have a chat with you.'

'What about?' I asked, knowing full well, but praying it was something different.

'I'll let Fiona speak to you.'

When Fiona walked in, I felt like I was back in school. Hanging my head in shame, I waited for her to drop the bad news.

''Tesha, is it correct you have a court date looming and you attacked a girl?' she asked, her eyes pleading with me that it wasn't true.

The guilt was written all over my face. I burst into tears and could barely speak.

'Oh my God, I'm sorry!' I cried. 'I didn't know how to tell you. I wanted to say something... but, I... but... I didn't know what to say.'

Fiona sighed. Understandably she looked pissed off. Of course this was the last thing she needed for her new show. All the crew and the channel had worked so hard to get this TV programme off the ground, now with a potential criminal in the cast you could see how that would scare off advertisers. Imagine all the wasted hours of footage that couldn't be used if I had to be edited out later. It would have cost them hundreds of thousands of pounds. I'll admit, back then I didn't know of any of the repercussions, I hadn't even thought about things like advertisers. I felt so awful when they started to explain the damage I had potentially caused by concealing the court case.

'Tell me everything that happened, Lateysha. From the beginning and leave nothing out,' Fiona said, looking worn out.

So I started from the beginning and told her everything I could remember. About my car being egged, how I confronted Paige in the bar that night, what happened during the fight, getting arrested in Swansea and the fact I was going to plead not guilty.

''Tesha,' she looked at me despairingly, 'how could you come into this house knowing you have a court date while you're here? Why didn't you tell us before?'

'I don't know!' I wept, 'I just thought I'd be able to keep it quiet. I didn't want to think about it, I suppose. I just thought I'd be able to come and go as I pleased. I didn't know we were locked in here for five weeks. I knew you wouldn't pick me to be on the show if I told you.'

Fiona didn't know what she was going to do. Not to blow smoke up my own behind, but she knew I was one of the best characters in the house and she didn't want to have to let me go.

As it happened, my solicitor confirmed the court date had been postponed until September, which was great news because it meant I could stay in the house until the end of the series.

I was made to stay in the crew apartment for a couple of days and then I spent some time back at home with my mum until it was finally decided if I could go back on the show. It was good to be back home, I didn't realise how much I'd missed everyone. Being in that mad house made me appreciate my family a little more. Luckily, I was allowed to return but only because the court case wouldn't begin until long after I'd finished filming.

The next scene I was involved in was when all the girls came to Port Talbot to convince me to rejoin the house. I very much doubt anyone in the house apart from Nicole would have cared if I came back, but on screen they all did their best play-acting at wanting me to return.

Obviously, bad news travels fast and by the time I got back into the house all the cast had heard Jade's version of events. I explained to everyone what had happened with Paige, the way it actually happened and not Jade's complete pack of lies. Luckily, they were all supportive.

Anyway, for the rest of the series I did my best to put it out my mind and got back to filming the show.

The series continued much as it had begun for me, with more arguments with the lads. I suppose you could say I caused trouble for myself, but at the time I didn't think so.

One of the worst moments was when Aron pulled some random

girl and decided to bring her back to the house. As far as Nicole was concerned, Aron was hers and she felt slighted. We were smashed and thought it would only be right to trash Aron's bed because he'd acted like a complete dickhead.

It was Nicole's idea, but she was 'my sister from another mister' and I wasn't about to let her gain revenge on her own. We decided to get the bin out of the girls' room, which was overflowing with tampons, cotton buds, face wipes, crisp and other food wrappers, and tip it onto his bed. Honestly, it was disgusting! The pair of us emptied everything out onto his mattress and then poured a bottle of Coke all over it for good measure.

It served him right, we reasoned. One minute he was all over Nicole and the next he was sticking his dick in some girl. To be honest, we acted like a pair of psychos, but at least it made good television. Liam was the first one to spot what we had done, and when he did, all hell broke loose. He came into our room screaming in our faces, before throwing a glass of water over Nicole. When he did that, I instantly saw red. Who the fuck did he think he was? I was tamping!

My modelling career on the show had pretty much come to a halt too. There was me thinking I was going to be on the covers of all the glossy magazines but the next modelling job I had was in an old man's snooker hall, draped over that gormless E.T. lookalike Chidgey. When I think back, it was hilarious. AK, our boss, kept saying, 'Imagine he is the man of your dreams', but he made my skin crawl! The closer she made me get, the more I wanted to be sick on him. I was looking stunning in the photos too, so I was raging that this whole shoot was about him. Honestly, I would rather have had Carley shove Aron's dirty boxers in my face again (like she did in episode 4) than pretend to kiss Chidge! I wish I could have whipped my weave in his face.

The last episode was the culmination of five tough weeks in the house. We had all been working towards an event that was being put on at Glam nightclub. It was billed as my chance to show the world what a goddess I was. I don't actually think I'm a goddess – I was simply playing up to my diva-esque image.

That evening, my role was to showcase some sexy underwear for all the clubbers. I was wearing a leopard print two-piece and everyone agreed I was looking lush. As soon as I got out there on the stage, I knew this was what I wanted to do for the rest of my life. It was kind of like a lightbulb moment. I don't know why I've always been confident being on a stage in just my underwear. For many women this would be their worst nightmare, but I loved being the centre of attention and stripping off. It reminded me too of the time when I was thrown out of school for giving that lap dance, which still makes me laugh.

The night in Glam was virtually my last night in Cardiff and now I had to face the harsh reality of life back in Port Talbot. I was delighted to be part of the series and at that time there was nothing in the world I would rather have done. And I felt like I'd really grown on the show and learnt a lot about myself – I wasn't the same girl, walking out those lime green doors, who'd first walked in, that's for sure. I felt I'd really grown as a person. Most people go to university to live with other people and get to know strangers, and in a way *The Valleys* was like that for me. I'd matured and I felt focused, because for the first time in my life I felt like I could make a future for myself. I could actually see light at the end of the tunnel.

Despite our ups and downs over the course of the series, I was going to miss most of the cast, but especially Nicole. I had made an amazing true friend in her and I knew I could trust her with my life. That kind of friendship doesn't come around very often and so when it does, cling to it. There comes a point in your life when you realise who really matters, who never did, and who always will.

Chapter Nineteen

ALL ALONE

After we had filmed Season One, I was given a list of potential managers, with phone numbers by the side of them. I scoured the list, looking for the names of companies I recognised, and for some reason I decided on a guy called Matt from United Agents. He would now be in charge of making me some money from my profile. I hoped he was as good as he said because at that point I had virtually nothing to my name. All the cast received the same amount of money. We weren't paid a fortune to do the show and with that, I had to pay all my bills.

Ryan, as you would probably expect, finished with me. He had made his decision when I was in the house and had started seeing someone else already. Apparently a girl I knew told him I'd been sending naked pictures of myself to all the Swansea football players while I was away, which wasn't true because I wasn't even allowed a mobile phone in the house. He chose to believe her and it didn't take him long to move on. So much for the last five years, huh?

The producers had hoped Ryan would come visit me in the house, but when they called, he said, 'No, I won't be there to visit 'Teesha. The circumstances have changed and we are not together.' They kept this from me until I came out and could speak to him myself. I rang him about a million times, but he wasn't answering. After a few hours I finally got hold of him and we agreed to meet.

When I saw him again, it was one of the most emotional times of my life. We both sat in my little blue mini, crying and reminiscing about old times.

'I can't believe this is the end, Ryan, after five years together!' I sobbed.

'I know, 'Teesha. It's so sad. I thought I was going to marry you!' he wept. 'I wanted to have kids with you.'

'So did I. I thought we would be together forever.'

'It's just not meant to be, 'Teesh.'

'What will we do about the house?' I sniffed, as I wiped the mascara away from my eyes.

'I've already said my friend can live there. He's been living with me while you've been away.'

'Great, so now I'm single and I've got nowhere to live! Thanks a lot, Ry, but then again, I have no money to pay the rent, so I suppose I've got no choice.'

''Teesh, what did you expect?'

But I didn't say anything. I suppose I didn't know what I expected Ryan to do after I cast him aside for a TV show, but I was hurt by the fact he'd moved on so quickly. He was my boyfriend and best friend, despite how shitty we might have been to each other. It upset me that I'd been abandoned by someone close to me. Again.

When he left, my upset changed to anger and I was absolutely raging. Now, I had nowhere to live, no boyfriend and no money. I felt like I had no one again. Luckily, my friend Harrison let me stay at his house for a few nights, but I didn't want to outstay my welcome and other nights I would have to sleep on my grandpa's floor.

I didn't think my life would end up like this after going on a glam TV show.

My mum wouldn't let me move back home. She had finally got rid of me and now said she had no room for me because she still had all my siblings in the house. There was barely enough room for them, she couldn't have me too. I suspect it was because she had a new man in her life, called Justin, and she didn't want me around, cramping her style. For that, I will never forgive her. It was the roughest time of my life and she didn't want me to be at home with her. Basically, I was living in my car, with practically my whole wardrobe in the boot. I'd become a nomad, constantly living out of a bag. I couldn't believe how she was behaving. I had stuck by her through all those shitty men she had brought into my life and been moved from pillar to post, but now that I really needed some support from her, she wasn't there.

After all the excitement of being on a reality show, I was now crashing back down to earth with an almighty thud. I thought my life was going to be different after filming, but it was worse than before. There I was, getting my head down on an old rusty coloured carpet in my grandpa's house, in a dusty sleeping bag. It wasn't at all what I expected and proved a really low point for me.

Eventually, after weeks of moving around constantly between my friends' houses, I found a flat I could rent. My old boss Jenny from the energy company was relocating to Liverpool and said I could have her flat at a good price. It would cost me £400 a month, which would be a struggle, but what choice did I have? I couldn't carry on living out of bags all my life. So, I took her up on the offer and used my savings to pay the first instalment. I would pay the next few months with money I would receive, hopefully, from being on *The Valleys*. Although we only received a relatively small amount at that stage from the actual filming, I was hoping to earn money from personal appearances in nightclubs. Although I didn't have any booked in, my agent Matt had promised to get a few bookings to tide me over.

At this point I still hadn't officially finished filming the show. I was in constant touch with MTV, because I was involved in green screen for the narrative of the show. As most *Valleys* fans will know, we do one-on-one pieces to camera to explain what we were thinking in the particular scene. Most viewers probably think we are still there and just slag each other off. Some of the things we say are really funny, too funny for some of the cast to have ever conjured up themselves. Sorry to shatter some dreams here, but when we're recording green screen a producer tells us what scene they want us to talk about and then we deliver the content in our own style, otherwise I'd never be able to remember every single thing that happened. Green screen is actually the most tiring part of the show because sometimes you have to say the same line over and over. Why? This can be for many reasons. Your hand actions aren't right or your facial expressions weren't good enough. Maybe you fluffed the line. Not enough energy, too much energy. Not forceful enough, not enough emotion... you get the picture. Believe me, it's a long and dull, repetitive process.

It was only a few weeks after we finished filming when the show was due to air but because of my court case, MTV made two versions of the first episode. One version featured me quite heavily and the other one was with me hardly in it at all. The outcome of the court case would be the deciding factor on which episode they would broadcast. Which is why, when they screened the show for the first time to the media in early September 2012,

I didn't attend, unlike the rest of the cast. I'm sure I was greatly missed. That afternoon I tweeted, saying I was too ill to attend, to throw any reporters off the scent.

About two hours later, I'd completely forgotten, though (you should know by now I have the memory of a goldfish!). Instead I uploaded a photo of myself in some new underwear I'd just bought. I thought nothing of the harmless tweet until I took a call from one of the producers, furious because I clearly didn't look ill in the snap. It was a genuine mistake, but he went wild and made me remove the photo.

'How dare you disrespect us by uploading a photo of you in your bra when we are having this huge press day!' the guy screamed.

'I'm sorry, I didn't even think,' I protested.

'Well, you need to *start* thinking! We've been covering for you, saying you're ill, and this is how you repay us?'

He was so angry.

'Shit, I'm sorry! I didn't mean it, I just forgot,' I explained.

True, my memory is appalling. I didn't upload the photo maliciously, I was just not thinking.

'Wake up, Lateysha! You need to start realising how your actions affect other people. Remove the photo and stay quiet on your Twitter!' he raged, before hanging up.

I felt really awful for a while afterwards. The team at MTV were doing everything they could to keep me on the show and I didn't want to do anything to make them even madder at me. I started to reflect on my actions a bit more after that, and realised I was causing chaos. I ws truly sorry for everything I'd done.

Chapter Twenty

MY DAY IN COURT

When my court date came round on 20 September 2012, I was the most nervous I've ever been in my whole life. I couldn't get to sleep; I kept thinking and worrying about the outcome. After all, I was taking a big risk in letting this go to trial. I could quite easily have pleaded guilty to the offence, but it would have been a lie. If anything, I kept thinking, *Why didn't I go to the police first? It was Paige who assaulted me.*

The next day, when I was getting ready for court, I was thinking, *I'm nineteen years old, what the fuck am I doing, going to court for attacking a girl?* But I had no answers. My life was completely out of control and I vowed to make a change when all this was over.

I wanted to dress down that day; I didn't want to bring any more attention to myself, so I wore a long black dress, black tights, court shoes and a cardigan. My friends, Harrison, Casey and Ellis, all had to come with me because they'd been witnesses and even if they hadn't, I know they would have been there to show their support anyway.

As I walked around the corner towards Swansea Crown Court, I saw two paparazzi photographers waiting to snap frames of me. I was so embarrassed; I don't even know how they found out about the case. Honestly, I wouldn't have put it past Paige or one of her pals to tip them off.

Entering the courtroom, I saw Paige and all her family staring at me, giving me evils, while the judge told the usher to bring in the jury. As they walked in, they gazed at me. There was a mixture of ages and sexes; they all just looked like everyday people.

One of the jury members was holding a notebook and pen and I saw her write something in it as soon as she sat down. The judge now asked if the jury was sworn in and if any of them knew me in the dock. Once they had all said 'no', the trial began.

I sat like a criminal behind glass until eventually I was called to give evidence in the witness box. It was a horrible experience, I was shaking and my lips were trembling. I could feel all the eyes of the courtroom on me. As I turned to my friends, they gave me a concerned smile. Paige's family sat there, stone-faced.

I tried to answer the questions as best I could, but Paige's barrister, Dean Pulling, ripped me apart. Standing my ground, I told the absolute truth about what had happened that night and I began by stating my actions were purely in self-defence.

He asked me about the Facebook message I'd written on my page, in which I'd said I was 'going to make her life hell'. Now, I know it was a stupid thing to write, but I was just so angry after what she'd written about me. I didn't actually mean what I said, and there was no threat to harm her physically. Yeah, I could have egged her car in return and/or gone to the police, but to be honest, I didn't want the drama.

The barrister continued to talk about the evening of the fight and I held my hands up to the point he made about confronting

Paige in a nightclub. It wasn't the best place to do it, although that's the beauty of hindsight, isn't it? But that was neither here nor there; the point was, had I been the one to start the fight? When that question was posed to me I answered honestly and told the court it was Paige who became aggressive and pulled my hair first.

My barrister, Stephen Rees, asked me, 'Were you wearing hair extensions?' To which I answered, 'Yes, they ended up on the floor.'

I told the court about Paige digging her nails into my eyes and explained that this was the only reason I'd bitten her.

My barrister said, 'She claimed you were hanging on like a dog so her leg was bleeding. Was it like that?' At that point, I shook my head before saying, 'No, I didn't bite hard – it was just for a few seconds.'

The next thing I was quizzed about was the apparent attack I'd made on Paige outside the club, which was a complete fabrication on her part. Yeah, we'd had crossed words, but we didn't fight. She just made herself look like an idiot for lying to the police in her statement.

After the hearing, the jury retired to make up their minds about the case. Whispering could be heard throughout the courtroom. All the jurors came back inside now after taking three hours to come to a decision. It was a nail-biting moment for everyone.

When he sat, the judge asked the foreman of the jury, a middle-aged man who was dressed really smartly, to stand. I was clenching my fists and I could feel my heart beating fast in my chest. The courtroom was on edge, you could have heard a pin drop. I could see my mates all huddled together, while Harrison had his forehead on Casey's shoulder, the tension too much to cope with.

The judge then read out the charges and asked what the verdict was. The foreman cleared his throat and glanced at the paper in front of him. It was as if there was an overly long pause, like Dermot O'Leary does on *The X Factor* to create some suspense and drama.

'Not guilty,' said the man. I looked around the courtroom. Had I heard him correctly? My head spun round to look at my friends, who were all beaming back at me, and I then realised my name had been cleared.

I looked over at the foreman and with tears in my eyes, mouthed a 'thank you' to him and the rest of the jury.

The first person to call me afterwards was Manus Wynne from True North. He was delighted with the outcome because now they could use the original episode, which featured me heavily. I remember him being so relieved. However, the cast weren't very supportive. They were all really annoyed that the show had been held back for three weeks while the outcome of the case was decided. Only Nicole got in contact to congratulate me on finally clearing my name. The court case made the papers, too. Local and national. And they used the hideous photos of me walking into court looking confused. They are still on the Internet now – I hate them!

That evening, I felt like an entire weight had been lifted. It was an astonishing relief for it all to be finally over. I didn't know what the future held for me, but I was kind of happy not knowing.

My life had turned a corner and for the first time in months, I slept soundly.

Chapter Twenty-one

BACKLASH

T V companies will attempt to prepare you for the worst-case scenarios regarding your newfound fame. Before we joined the cast of *The Valleys*, we were given the 'Talk of Doom' and assessed by psychologists. The Talk of Doom is where a producer will sit you down and explain, quite bluntly, that when the show airs you may be hated, the press may dig up things you don't like, you could be the victim of abuse and audiences may react badly to the show, but that's the risk you take in putting yourself out there. Meanwhile, psychologists assessed our mental states to see if we were mentally capable of taking all they could throw at us.

They also gave us media training and told us what to expect in our press interviews. We were advised not to reveal too much information about the production process of making the show. They also helped us by providing stock answers if a journalist ever posed those tricky kinds of questions.

'*Is the show set up?*' No, absolutely not. We just say and do whatever we want. They capture all footage and edit it all together later. (Kind of true.)

'*Is the show scripted?*' No, it's not. We are never told what to say, not even in green screen. (Largely true, except during green screen we were given pointers and directions as to what we should say.)

'*Are the romances real?*' Of course they are! We couldn't fake being nice to someone for that length of time. (My romantic dalliances *were* real by the way.)

'*Do you find the camera intrusive?*' No, we never know they're there. We just forget we are being filmed. (You try waking up to a camera twelve inches from your face!)

It was our job to make the show as successful as possible. We couldn't shatter the illusion for the audiences, who all thought everything on screen was 100 per cent real.

Armed with our stash of media answers, we travelled to London to do our press day on 24 September 2012. I suppose it was only then that I began to feel like a star and that this was actually all happening for real.

The morning started with a photo shoot in the Docklands. I'd borrowed a tight purple body-con dress from one of my pals because I had no money for anything new. I wore huge beige heels and my bleached hair had to be the same blonde as on the series for continuity, even though I absolutely hated it by then.

The day was crazy; there were sheep running around, which had been sprayed with *The Valleys* logo, while we were made to pose in front of an army of paparazzi. Flash bulbs were going off everywhere as I stood and blew kisses to the men with cameras. And for the first time I felt like a proper bona-fide celeb. It was what I'd been waiting for my whole life and I was glad it was finally happening.

Later that afternoon, we split up into little groups and we were taken around all the magazine offices in London (I went to *Heat* and *Reveal*). I took the journalists cupcakes and sweet-talked them, hoping they would feature me positively whenever they were writing about the show. They asked me the questions the media department had prepared me for, and like the good little starlet I was, I trotted my pre-rehearsed answers out.

I didn't have a clue how I would be portrayed on screen; I could barely remember anything that had been filmed. So when I watched the first episode with all the other housemates in the MTV offices in London, I was excited and nervous at the same time. We sat there laughing, waiting for our new show to be thrown up on the huge screen. Of course we were all dying to see it, but no sooner had it aired than the mood in the room turned completely awkward.

In our green screen interviews we had all been slagging each other off, big style. As soon as we heard our sound bites, everyone began to cringe. I was really slating Jenna, Liam and Carley, and I could tell they were hurt by my comments. Plenty of them had their own spiteful words to say about me, though, so I guess it was just swings and roundabouts. Luckily, no one seemed to take anything to heart because we all realised that we were making a TV show.

It was pretty shocking to see the show and how it had all been edited together; it was so rude and vulgar. I worried about how the general public were going to react, also what my family would say.

Speaking of family, when the show premiered on 25 September 2012, my mum called me in floods of tears.

''Teysha, I can't believe it,' she wailed. 'I can't believe you're having sex on TV!'

'Mum, calm down! I didn't have sex on TV.'

'I'm so disappointed, I'm so upset,' she kept on repeating.

'Mum, I didn't have sex on TV. I just got in bed with Leeroy. Nothing happened.'

'Everyone from Port Talbot has been talking about the show and now you're going to be a laughing stock, 'Teysha.'

'I don't care what people think, Mum. Let them say what they want.'

'I'm sorry, Lateysha, but I'm so ashamed of you right now.'

'Oh, for fuck's sake! I can't deal with you, Mum, you're making me feel bad. I'll talk to you tomorrow,' I told her, and with that, I hung up.

I couldn't help but feel sorry for my mum, but I couldn't turn the clock back now. I don't ever regret doing *The Valleys*, but what I do regret is how I behaved on the show, and if I did it again, maybe I would tone it down a little. Mum had watched the first fifteen minutes, which showed a clip of me climbing into bed with Leeroy. Had she seen the rest of it, she would have realised I didn't actually have sex with him. All we did was cwtch.

The same evening, we all went out together to DSTRKT in London. I remember thinking, *Oh, my God, we're famous!* All night, I kept checking my Twitter on my phone. It was so exciting to watch my Twitter count rise – sad, right? But it was still pretty cool.

I half expected to get all these wonderful messages from people telling me how great they thought the show was and how fab I looked on screen, but nothing could have been further from the truth. All I received was mountains of abuse. People were saying, 'Oh, my God, she's fucking hanging!', 'Who the fuck does she think she is?' and 'She looks like Beyoncé's big toe', to name just a few.

I remember thinking, *Fuck what have I done? Why did I even bother to sign up to this TV show?* I thought I was going to be the one everyone liked, but I was actually the most hated housemate. I wasn't happy about the way I'd been portrayed on the show, but it was too late. Now, I just had to ride it out and think what will be, will be.

The biggest backlash came from the Welsh people, who said we had completely embarrassed the country; they absolutely hated the show. There we were, thinking we were going to be these massive celebrities and we had no idea we would be so detested. The thing is, what the older Welsh crowd didn't realise is that what we were doing was no different to what other young kids get up to every single day of their lives. The only difference was we were being filmed doing it. I always say reality shows are more like a mirror than a window and if they didn't like what we were doing, they didn't like what was going on in society as a whole. Kids I know are worse than what you see us getting up to on screen.

I know the TV company tried to prepare us for the worst, but really nothing anyone says can make you feel better when you receive death threats and abuse every single minute of the day. I didn't even want to leave my flat. Ever. I remember one of the producers, Natalie Grant, called me and I just broke down in floods of tears about some of the nasty comments I had received. It was one of the shittiest times of my life and my confidence and self-esteem were shot to pieces.

As I said, I was the most hated person on the whole show. The most abuse was always thrown at me on Twitter. I came across as the bitchy, stuck-up, arrogant one in the group and I didn't go down well with girls or guys. Also, I was the least popular in terms of marketability, which meant I wasn't getting any money from the show. No one wanted to book me for anything and basically, the whole time sucked.

It was then that I decided to change managers and take my career into my own hands. I had heard good things about an organisation called Inked-up Management, who also looked after Jenna. But when Jenna found out I was in talks with them she threatened to leave if they signed me (I think she was jealous of the competition). Which is when I met with Luke Mills from Misfits Management. Young, fresh and full of ideas, he had many reality stars on his books and filled me with confidence about my new career.

When I watched the series as a whole, I couldn't believe I'd been such a diva and so bitchy at times. I'm not at all like that in real life. All I will say on the matter is the girl you see on screen is a very skewed version of myself. At the time I was playing up to an image I thought the audience would love but it just did not work.

Don't get me wrong, I do take responsibility for my own actions – after all, it was my choice to put myself in front of the lens. I had wanted to be on screen so badly that I was willing to do anything. In some ways, I was like a lamb to the slaughter... or perhaps more aptly, a sheep to *The Valleys*.

Chapter Twenty-two

BLASTS FROM THE PAST

When my dad, Leroy Henry, saw I was on *The Valleys*, he started to take an interest in me. Surprise, surprise! He would call me up a few times and say how gorgeous I looked on TV. By this point he had split with Farrah. Rumour has it he was treating her badly, which I can fully imagine he did, given the brutal attack he launched on my brother all those years ago.

'I'm so proud of you, Lateysha. I always knew you would be a star,' he would say. 'You look stunning with your blonde hair – I can't believe you are my daughter sometimes.'

'Thanks, Leroy,' I would say. I never called him 'Dad' anymore. As far as I was concerned he wasn't my father; I have never had one.

'So, now you are a big star, you must be making a good living for yourself?'

'Not really,' I would say, non-committal.

'Ha, ha!' he would laugh, 'I bet you're doing better than your old dad, huh?'

'I doubt it,' I said. I was short and snappy with him because I just wanted him off the phone.

'Well, you know if you could help your dad out I would pay you back, 'Teysha.'

'Sorry, Leroy, I can't. I have no money to give you,' I told him. Which was true. I didn't have any spare cash. 'I have to go now, I'll talk to you soon.' And with that, I hung up.

It's funny how he came crawling out of the woodwork when he saw I was on TV and presumed I was making money. He thought he could call me up and guilt-trip me into giving him cash. But where was he when I was growing up? Where were the birthday cards, the Christmas cards, the phone calls? As far as I was concerned, he could fuck off! I would never give him a penny of my hard-earned cash. He didn't care about me for years, so now he's not got the privilege of having me in his life. I know he doesn't love Regan or me; he can't do because he doesn't even know us.

Not long after that phone call I texted him, telling him he was going to die a lonely old man. None of his kids would care about him or be there at his funeral. He got pretty angry with me and replied, saying, don't speak to me like that. But it's the honest truth. I've giving up trying to have a relationship with that man. I hope he reads this book and realises just what I think of him and what a wonderful opportunity he has missed by not getting to know me or Regan.

I was about to have another row, with another man from the past, too. But this one wasn't so easy as just slamming down the phone.

Nicole asked me to meet her for a drink one afternoon. She

sounded quite upset and distant on the phone, which was unusual for her.

'I need to ask you something and just please tell me the truth,' she said.

I knew what was coming.

'Just please, please, be honest with me.'

I looked her in the eye, took a deep breath and sighed.

'OK...'

'Did Antony get you pregnant?' she asked, her eyes pleading with mine. I don't know who told her, but the rumour was doing the rounds in South Wales and you can never keep anything secret for long. I knew this conversation was going to be difficult, so I would have to do it quickly, like pulling off a plaster.

'Yes, he did.' I felt awful as soon as the words left my mouth. 'But I don't really want to talk about it, Nicole. I mean, I'm still upset I had to go through an abortion.'

Nicole looked devastated, with tears in her eyes. 'Thanks for telling me,' she said. 'You are such a good friend and I know that can't have been easy.'

I was relieved the secret was finally out, but I felt terrible for Nicole.

'I fucking hate him, 'Teesh!' she cried. But I could tell this was hurting her so much because she was still in love with him. To see her so distraught was hurting me too. It's awful when your loved ones are upset, and to know you are the cause of it is even worse.

She texted Antony straight away, saying, 'I can't believe you didn't tell me you got Lateysha pregnant.'

And his reply: 'She's fucking lying.'

He really was a piece of shit. Why would I lie to my best friend over something so devastating as an abortion by her ex-boyfriend? Immediately we rang him back and Nicole put me on the phone to tear a strip off him. We got into a huge argument and in the end I showed Nicole all the texts and Facebook messages to prove it to her.

'I fucking hate him! I am never speaking to him again, he's a fucking pig!' she raged.

'Nic, he made me pay for it all myself. He didn't give me a penny towards it. He ignored my Facebook messages, all my texts. He's a complete dick! You are better off without him,' I told her.

'You're right, I know,' she sobbed. 'I never want anything to do with him again!'

Famous last words…

Chapter Twenty-three

TWO'S UP

For Series Two I decided to change my look. I adopted a stunning platinum blonde weave. I'd been working hard to lose a bit of weight through eating carefully, cutting down on the booze and going for longer jogs. And by making a few simple changes, I had lost 6lb.

I'd also bagged myself a hot new boyfriend called Calum, who had a ridiculous number of tattoos. I think it was because he was so unusual-looking he caught my eye. He was a bit strange and everyone needs a bit of strange at some point in life. I met him in a club in Watford. As soon as he walked in, I thought he was stunning – I fancied him so much, I couldn't even talk to him. I sent my friend Ellis over to bring him to my table and I was literally in love. Not long after we started dating and it was a complete whirlwind romance. We had only been together for three months when I was due to go back in *The Valleys*. I was devastated to be leaving him for so long, but I promised to be a good girl while I was away and this time I meant it.

Series Two brought with it some cast changes. Aron was given the boot on the day we began filming. Having packed his stuff ready for the next six weeks, he came all the way to Cardiff only to be told he wasn't part of the series anymore. He was inconsolable at the time and I didn't like the way he was just booted off the show completely without warning. It was a lesson to the rest of us too, that at any moment any one of us could be kicked off without a decent reason. I suppose Aron hadn't really impacted on the group as much as he could and they just didn't see him gelling with us in the second series. I hear he's doing really well for himself now. He's still doing his kick-boxing and runs his own personal training business. I'm glad for him too, because the lad didn't have a bad bone in his body.

In his place came two new cast members, Jason and Anthony Suminski. They were ape-like, identical twins and when I first met them, I thought they were ridiculously hot. Which is just typical – as soon as I got a boyfriend I didn't actually want to cheat on, they brought in two half-decent-looking lads! But the only person I would be kissing would be my lesbi partner in crime Nicole and it didn't take long for us to lock lips, either. On our first night out in Cardiff, we were necking on like it was going out of fashion.

It's not cheating if you kiss a girl mate, is it?

Meanwhile, I had started to build up some decent images in my portfolio and I was looking forward to continuing my career as a model. I was literally buzzing for my first shoot but as with everything on our show, it didn't exactly go to plan. It was a Tarzan and Jane theme revolving around the new boys and Jenna. I was tamping when I found out. Why wasn't I the Jane? And worse than that, they made me wear an elephant suit. Were they serious? The trunk made me look like I had a big grey cock on my head! It should have been me freezing my tits off, flaunting my body in skimpy leopard underwear.

Of course I knew the real reason, because it was funnier for the audiences to see me raging and that's why the producers constantly put me in these positions. I know it wasn't AK, our resident photographer, or Jenna in control of the shoot, but I would still kick off, like I was supposed to. I would stick to the plan.

Jenna wasn't a better model than me. All fake boobs and hair, there's no sex appeal there. She didn't have a clue what she was doing in front of the camera. On screen it looked like I was being made to look a fool by AK and she was literally howling at the sight of me in that elephant costume. I couldn't wait for the shoot to be over and I just prayed the next time I was in front of the lens, I would be the one commanding all the attention.

I was looking forward to a chilled night after having such a shitty day, standing around like Dumbo, but the twins had other ideas. They decided it would be hilarious to have a food fight in the middle of the kitchen. Don't get me wrong, I'm always up for a bit of fun, but when they started throwing red chilli sauce onto my new white-blonde, luscious locks I was seriously raging.

My hair had cost me hundreds of pounds and many long, boring hours in the salon to get it to look this good. Well, it would have cost me hundreds of pounds but I actually managed to wangle a freebie in return for advertising on my Twitter. Now those two piss-drinking gorillas had ruined it with red chilli sauce. I was terrified it was going to be stained, but luckily I washed it in time. Now, I know it sounds ridiculous but I was absolutely devastated when they did that. I had literally been in the house a few days and already my new look was destroyed. Everyone knows how protective I am over my hair. You can mess around with me all you want, but don't ever touch my weave!

Of course I got my own back. Those newcomers needed to know you don't mess with Queen Lateysha. The girls and I ransacked the bin and found some stinking horrible dead fish. Again, they were strategically placed by the producers but we went along with the idea because we knew it would be hilarious to film.

The smell was beyond revolting; I was retching with it in my hands. So, we decided to hide our decomposing fish in their pillows so the room would be honking for the rest of the series. We literally smeared fish guts in their blankets until the room stunk to high heaven! I know that sounds horrible, but they needed to be taught a lesson. As you would expect, when the lads found out, they were seriously pissed off. The crew were buzzing because it was causing controversy within the group, and let's be honest, that's exactly what the viewers wanted to see, although no one wanted to film in their bedroom any more – it was like Swansea fish market!

But we weren't there for food fights and fish hiding; often we had to get on with work. Let's not forget we were all in Cardiff to better our careers. The next day, I had a photo shoot with AK. I made sure I had an early night, but it really didn't matter because the next day we were about to endure the worst weather imaginable. It was a freezing cold winter's morning, minus two degrees, to be exact. The crew had organised an ice-cream truck to be driven to the house, which was to be used as a backdrop. With any photo shoot there's a lot of waiting around and when you're also being filmed for a TV show the process takes even longer. I was wearing skimpy knickers and a bra and honestly, I've never felt so cold in all my life! My teeth would not stop chattering, my fingernails were going blue. I was made to pose in front of an ice-cream truck, sucking on a 99 cone. There was chocolate sauce all over my boobs, whipped cream, hundreds and thousands floating around in my knickers, and all the while you could have hung coats on my nipples. It was horrendous! Still, like a true professional, I under-promised and over-delivered. The shots were amazing when I saw them. Some of the other girls shied away from getting covered in food, but not me. Put it this way, I like to get dirty!

After I'd warmed up back in the house, I realised what great, fun shots they would turn out to be. Yes, doing it was the worst, but I was hopeful the results would look amazing and really boost the images in my glamour-modelling portfolio. With that in mind, I was ready to party so we all headed to Cardiff's hottest club, Glam. I was still so proud of myself that ever since I'd been in Cardiff I'd never even so much as thought about another guy. There I was, in a club with wall-to-wall fit fellas, and I wasn't interested in any of them. It was such a change from Series One and it made me realise just how much I loved my boyfriend. I must have been looking stunning that night because even Chidgey tried it on with me, though. He kept grabbing my face and pulling me towards him. Of course I shoved him away. I mean, what was he thinking? I had a fit boyfriend back home and even if I hadn't, the last man on earth I would choose to get with would be Chidge! The opposite of my type, he reeked of desperation. I don't know what he was on that night, but he ended up throwing a drink all over my hair and ruining my eye make-up. I don't think he meant it maliciously, but don't these guys know my weave is my fucking life? What's so hard to understand about that? Do NOT touch my hair – EVER! It was the wrong side of enough.

Now I will explain why the title of this book is *Valleywood*. Remember in Series One, when we all got those sheep tattooed on our foofs? Well, I hated mine ever since the moment it was first scratched into my mound. I wanted it covered, and after much deliberation decided on 'Valleywood'. I'm from the Valleys, with all the glamour of Hollywood, so what could be better? The tattooist had designed the script like it had been written in red lipstick to match my famous pillar-box rouge lips. I loved it as soon as I saw it, but having it inked was another matter altogether. If you've ever had a tattoo on your nether regions, you will know just how excruciating the pain can be, and if you haven't, don't bother! Luckily, Nicole came with me to hold my hand, but I would never recommend getting font on your foof. Trust me on this one. Although when the tattoo was done, I absolutely loved it. I thought it was completely stunning, which might sound crazy, but I kept thinking, *I'll be getting my fanny out even more now!*

Series Two was going really well. In the first series there'd been some friction between the girls, but since then we had all grown quite close. I had hated Carley and Natalee in the beginning, but you know what? They are the coolest girls! I count them as my best friends now, along with Nicole.

So, like I said, all the cast got on well enough... until one of us had something better than anyone else. I don't like to think I'm the jealous type, but when Jenna got a modelling opportunity with one of Britain's best-selling lads' mags, *Nuts*, I was devastated. In my opinion I was a better model than her, but because she had that blow-up sex doll look, she was getting more opportunities than me. When AK told us the news, I couldn't help but feel jealous. I was completely tamping and as far as I was concerned, it was AK's fault I wasn't getting these golden opportunities. She made me look like an idiot in half the shoots, while Jenna got to dress up in sexy underwear. It wasn't fair! I know I should have been happy for Jenna, but I wasn't. Not in the slightest. I couldn't even look her in the eye, knowing she was going to have her huge fake chest plastered all over the country, whereas I was still doing these idiotic shoots with AK.

Speaking of idiotic shoots, AK's next bright idea was to do a shoot solely focusing on hair and she wanted to turn mine into an Afro. I couldn't believe it! Why was everyone constantly trying to mess with my hair? I was about to scream. Did they not know how much money, time and effort I spend on my hair, trying to make it look different to an Afro? Honestly, I knew the producers were doing all this to wind me up and it was really getting on my tits!

Not only that, the next photo shoot AK had lined up involved me having to get sexy with a tarantula. When they brought out this big and hairy spider, I screeched. It looked like my foof just before a six-week wax! How the hell was I supposed to make this look sexy? Still, I was never going to beat Jenna in the cover-girl stakes if I didn't up my game. In the end I had two giant spiders crawling all over me. And if that wasn't bad enough, they brought out a huge, yellow python, which had to be draped all over me. Of course I was terrified but seeing how wimpy the other girls were getting was really off-putting and I didn't want to be like them. I had to get stuck in and get on with the job, I realised. Hopefully, the rest of the cast could see that I was taking my opportunities seriously and was not just on the show to mess around.

Our next task, as in the first series, was to try and put on a club night. Since my new tattoo had caused quite a stir, I had the bright idea of calling the night 'Valleywood' and in my head it was going to be the most glamorous party ever seen. The only problem was, the venue for this amazing night of booze and entertainment was in Jason and Anthony's hometown of Pontypridd. For those of you who have never set foot there, count yourselves lucky! It's one of the biggest dives in Wales. Why on earth we had to put the night on there was beyond me, but we had no choice in the matter and had to make the most of the situation.

Naturally, I wanted to be the star of the show, but I had to include at least a few of the others. It was decided Jason and

Anthony would be my backing dancers and to be honest, I had no choice in the matter, even though they performed like Dumb and Dumber.

The shoot for the posters was hilarious. AK took the entire group to a farm somewhere deep in the Valleys. Like most of our shoots, it was freezing! I was made to wear a stunning sequinned gold dress, cut down almost to my navel. My long locks were flowing in the breeze and you've guessed it, I had my famous red pout. As usual with our shoots, everyone was complaining too much about the freezing-cold temperatures to care about the photos, but if you want to be a top model, you just have to get on with the task in hand. I absolutely nailed those pictures, much to the annoyance of the rest of the cast. It wasn't my fault I was good at my job.

After witnessing my success, the lads thought they needed to bring me down a peg or two. I could hear them creeping up behind me and, instinctively, I ran as fast as I could. Although I carried on running just as fast as my wellies would take me, it was no use and they eventually caught up with me. Anthony picked me up. Screaming and wailing, I was trying to break free but I still ended up covered in a ton of cow shit. So, not only was I freezing cold and muddy but now my hair and face were covered in cow shit. Let me repeat that again, my *weave* was covered in cow shit! TAMPING. FUMING. RAGING.

I could do nothing but scream. Meanwhile, my heart was going like the clappers. I was going crazy, but all anyone else could do was laugh uncontrollably. Now, I couldn't stop crying. I thought this shoot was meant to be glamorous and all the boys could do was ruin it. I had cow shit everywhere too. It was disgusting! Had the boys not learnt their lesson from when we hid rotten fish in their bedding? Do NOT touch my hair!

But the most awkward moment of Series Two happened when we were on a night out in Cardiff. Remember when I told you about Antony, Nicole's ex-boyfriend, who also got me pregnant? Well, Nicole had struck up a relationship with him again, despite my confession about the abortion. So much for all that 'I'll never see him again' talk, but if she could look past all the drama, so could I. What I found more difficult was when he was paraded in front of my face. He turned up in Swansea and I didn't know where to look.

My face dropped when he walked in. He had some nerve, showing up here on our show, knowing I would be there too. After the procedure he had blanked all my calls and got me into debt because he preferred to go on holiday rather than offer help with the payment. And now there he was, sat in front me like nothing had ever happened, kissing the face off my best friend!

I couldn't hide how uncomfortable I was feeling. Of course I knew the producers had invited him because they had heard I had shagged him in the past, but maybe they wouldn't have done so if I'd told them the full truth. He tried to say 'hello' to me, and I smiled casually back. I didn't want to be unfriendly, but Nicole knew why I was being off. I remember having to run off to the toilets because I began to get upset. It wasn't that he was now back with Nicole; I was happy for her if she was happy. But I thought he was so fucking cheeky the way he wasn't even sorry for how he had treated me back when I was pregnant – leaving me in the lurch like that and never contributing anything. Seeing him also brought back the memories of having the termination, which was never nice to think about and always made me upset. I try my hardest to make sure I never show my vulnerable side because I don't like anyone to know they've got to me, but that night I couldn't hold back and so I had a cry in the toilet cubicle while everyone else was partying. I should have been able to go to my best friend but for obvious reasons, I couldn't. Besides, I didn't want to hurt Nic any more and ruin her relationship. I was pretty sure Antony would somehow ruin it all by himself, so I would just have to wait until she eventually saw the light.

I don't think the viewers knew how close Nicole and I were. To call us best friends doesn't seem to describe us properly; we were more than that. Nothing was off-limits with us two. It's like when we went shopping for sex toys. Some friends might get a little shy talking about such things, but not us: we would literally use the toys on each other if we felt like it. Picking out dildos and playing with the bondage gear was one of the funniest moments while filming the show. We found a double-ended dildo that we were pretending to fuck. Then I donned a gimp mask and leathers, while Nicole found a vibrating strap-on. Dressed in all that garb we couldn't control ourselves and who knows what might have happened with a few drinks inside us? Luckily we were stone cold sober.

The other girls and guys in the group were jealous of how close Nicole and I were. No one else had anyone's back like we did. It was almost as if we could tell what the other one was thinking without even speaking, like telepathy.

The last shoot of the series was the best one yet. Jordan had decided he needed a new face for his nightclub, Glam. It was between Jenna, Natalee and myself. Whoever took the best photo, got the gig. I knew I'd performed well throughout the series with my modelling shots and I had to win this campaign. If I didn't, I might as well give up altogether.

The theme for this shoot was 'all fur coat, no knickers', which I took a little too literally. I was the only one out of the girls to actually do the shoot minus my thong. At least no one could say I wasn't dedicated to the cause! As always, I smashed it: I writhed around on the floor, making sure the fur covered those all-important bits, and literally made love to the camera. I felt like one of those hoochy girls in a rapper music video.

We didn't know who had been chosen until we actually had to appear at the nightclub, a few days later. I was praying it would be me and as I strolled round the corner of the club, I saw my hard work had paid off. There I was, on a huge billboard at the side of a club, looking absolutely lush! I couldn't believe how big the poster was, but seeing myself gloriously high just confirmed that I loved what I'd been doing. I loved modelling and I wanted to make it my full-time career. So what if Jenna got the first cover? Soon enough I would get my own cover, but that would just be the tip of the iceberg.

I screamed with delight when I saw the poster. Nicole was so happy for me – she knew how much I'd wanted this and was genuinely pleased about my success. Bowling over to Jordan, I hugged him so tight; I couldn't thank him enough. For me, this was the ultimate highlight of Series Two.

But like everything in life, what comes up, must go down.

The night after our 'Valleywood' performance, AK and Jordan came round to deliver some bad news: not everyone would be returning for the next series. The cast members gathered on the sofas to await the news. First in the firing line was Liam, who I couldn't have cared less about. But then they said they were firing Nicole because she didn't know what she was good at in terms of her career. Immediately, I burst into tears and so did Nicole. We were both heart-broken. It was like my heart had been ripped out and I vowed, one way or another, to get her back on the show.

Once again, the experience of filming the show had been bittersweet, but I hoped the audiences had loved it just as much as we had enjoyed shooting it. After we wrapped for another season, we had no idea if there would ever be a third. As always, I felt like we'd left it up to the powers that be to run the course of our lives, trusting they knew better than us. We all hoped and prayed a third series would be commissioned, but the viewing figures would eventually be the decider.

I came out the house excited to see my boyfriend, Calum. No contact for six weeks is really tough and I can't tell you how much I missed him. As soon as I got my phone back, I called him but he didn't answer. Instead, he texted me and was really distant. We agreed to meet up a few days later and instead of us being all over each other, it was really forced and awkward. He was acting all weird with his phone too – it was always face down and silent, just like Ryan used to do. I also noticed he'd been commenting on his ex-girlfriend's Instagram photos and eventually he confessed to still being in touch with her. I was absolutely gutted. We got into this huge row, but he reasoned that we had only been together for three months and we were too much of a new relationship for me to go off for six weeks and expect everything to be cool again when we met.

We ended that evening and I was deeply hurt by the rejection. I had really fallen for Calum and I thought he felt the same way about me. I'm big enough to admit to it when things get to me and being dumped again because of *The Valleys* was a bitter pill to swallow. It was almost as if these lads were using my dream job against me. I vowed then and there, if ever there was another series I would be going into that house footloose and fancy-free.

Chapter Twenty-four

YOU BEAUTIFUL

I'm a natural born performer; ask anyone. I have the confidence, drive, ambition and the kick-ass attitude to go with it. And I'm so modest too. Ha! So when I was approached to do a hit song with an American rapper in October 2013, I was absolutely thrilled and jumped at the chance. (Well, after I knew it was all above board and a legitimate offer, I *then* jumped at the chance!)

It's fair to say, I'm not the world's best singer but I can hold a tune. I have always wanted to go into music, ever since I was a little girl, so when a guy called D-Jukes contacted my agent, Luke Mills from Misfits Management, with a song he wanted me to feature on, I knew I wanted to be involved.

This guy had messaged me on Twitter a few times, saying he wanted us to work on a track together, but I never really took him seriously. I get all kinds of crazy messages on Twitter, so you must forgive me for not being bowled over at first. But after he contacted Luke with a legitimate proposal, we both thought it sounded like a good opportunity to push into the music industry. I hadn't made up my mind completely, but I asked D-Jukes to send me the track so I could come to a decision. He sent me the three-minute song via email and I opened it on my iPhone, not really knowing what to expect at first. I hadn't heard D-Jukes' music before, so I really was listening with an open mind. The song titled 'You Beautiful' featured his husky American voice against a simple, repetitive, catchy backing track.

As soon as I heard it, I couldn't get the song out of my head and I began singing it round my bedroom the whole day. Like I said before, I have the attention span of a goldfish, so for it to stick in my head was a good sign. If *I* could remember it, it was surely catchy enough to become a hit.

What really prompted me to say 'yes' to his offer was the fact that Series Three of *The Valleys* was looming. It had been commissioned again and I was buzzing that my profile seemed to be growing. I knew I would soon be getting a call from the producers, asking me what was going on in my life, and it would be pretty cool to turn round and say, 'I'm releasing a single.' None of the other cast mates were doing anything that could compare to that. Apart from a few modelling jobs they hadn't really ventured out and tried something new. But I've always been a great believer in 'fortune favours the brave' so I threw caution to the wind and agreed to feature on the track.

Sure enough, a week later, Manus Wynne, the senior producer of *The Valleys*, called, asking me about ideas for the third series. He was delighted to hear about me potentially releasing a single and promptly got in touch with D-Jukes to get the ball rolling.

After that, it all happened so fast. A week later I was on my way down to a recording studio in Glastonbury to meet D-Jukes for the first time and lay down the lyrics to our single. I'd been sent the words a few days earlier and had mastered them quite easily. There was nothing too challenging in the song. The only downside was that I felt I wasn't singing enough on it (I'm such a diva!).

When I arrived at the studio it was not at all what I expected. It was in a little village, with old people walking their dogs and nipping to the local post office. The studio itself looked like a garden shed at the back of the local community church – it certainly wasn't the kind of cutting-edge, high-tech office space you might imagine. It was more *Emmerdale* than Abbey Road. Still, I was there and just had to get on with the job in hand.

When I walked in it was pretty weird because D-Jukes and me had never met before. He was a tall, friendly black guy, wearing the requisite cool, baggy rappers' clothes and a snap-back. He was there with his stunning partner, Sophia, who is also a singer. Shortly afterwards, *The Valleys* film crew arrived and began to set up so they could film us both in the recording studio. The footage was then going to be used on the show to explain to viewers what I'd been doing since the end of last season.

If any of you have ever had the chance to record music in a recording studio, you'll know just how expensive every single minute can be, so after a quick introduction it was time for me to get into the booth and sing my parts of the song. There was no chance to get to know D-Jukes or his missus, or exchange any pleasantries, like how the journey was, their history in the music industry or what they hoped for the single. I was literally pushed into this small wooden booth with only a microphone and headphones inside. On one side there was a glass window so the music producers and *The Valleys* film crew could watch me singing, but other than that I was on my own.

From start to finish, it took me about an hour to record my parts of the song, which you'll agree is pretty quick, considering I had no idea what I was doing. Too quick, if you ask me! I wanted to savour the moment and really enjoy recording the single, but time and money wait for no man or woman – unless you're Mariah Carey or some other diva. The music producers wanted the track laid down as fast as humanly possible. But the producers were good and they knew exactly how they wanted the track to sound. If I messed up, or they wanted it to sound slightly different, they would tell me really clearly so I could nail it on my second attempt.

Call me big-headed but when I left the studio I knew I'd smashed it. I was confident the song was going to be a hit and I left feeling really happy with myself. All *The Valleys* crew were pleased with the footage they shot and they were singing the song by the time we left, which made me smile. At that point I couldn't wait to get back to filming and let everyone hear my monster smash!

A week after recording the song, I was sent the finished master copy of the track via email. When I heard it, I actually thought it sounded better than I could ever have expected. I was really proud of it; I couldn't wait for my friends to hear it too. But when I played it to Harrison, Casey and Ellis for the first time, they kind of looked at each other, not knowing quite what to say. Clearly, they didn't want to hurt my feelings, but I could tell by the looks on their faces, they hated it.

'Hmm, it's catchy!' said one.

'You sound… really…. great, 'Teesh,' said another.

I was gutted by their reaction; they could have just lied and told me they loved it, that's what I would have done. And if my best friends didn't like it, what would the rest of the housemates think? I'd gone from absolutely loving the thought of having a single out to now thinking I was making a huge fool of myself.

'You don't like it?' I asked my mates.

'Yeah, it's… different,' they lied. 'Really gets in your head, doesn't it?'

'A bit like that "Gangnam Style" did and look how big that went!'

'Thanks for all your support,' I sulked.

It was really my agent Luke who got me to see all the positives and made me realise that everyone has different taste in music. Some people were going to love it and others would hate it, that's just the way life is.

The single became a huge part of my storyline on Series Three of *The Valleys* and I got to perform it many times during our 'Valleywood' nights when we travelled around the country. However, the first time I played the track for my housemates, they reacted in just the same way as my friends.

The producers pulled me to one side and told me to go into the house with a pile of CDs I'd made, which had my face on the cover – more as a joke than anything else. They told me to bound into the room and say, 'Everyone, I have a surprise! I have a new track and I want you all to listen to it.' I knew it sounded cheesy, but of course I did as I was asked.

I put the CD on and as they started to listen, I felt awkward. They all just gazed around the room, looking sheepish. None of them wanted to give me any praise or slag me off to my face. I knew they would probably wait until green screen before they told me what they really thought of my music.

If you ask me, I think a huge part of it all was jealousy. It could have been a classic hit but still they wouldn't have admitted they liked it because none of the other housemates had anything substantial going on in their lives. Any one of them will tell you, if they're being honest, there's a lot of competitiveness between us all. No one likes to see anyone doing better than anyone else and they knew my song would be a big storyline for me. I knew it when I saw their faces – they were envious of my potential screen time.

Anyway, regardless of how they felt I was going to milk this musical opportunity for all it was worth.

The real fun happened when I got to shoot the video for the song. I mean, how many people can say they have released a single and shot a video that is going to be played on MTV? That alone was well worth it.

People will probably think I'm such an arrogant bitch because the title of the song is 'You Beautiful', but just to clear one thing up: I don't actually think I'm beautiful. I mean, I know I'm not ugly, but I'm not so big-headed that I think I'm Kim Kardashian or something. So when we came up with the concept for the video I wanted to poke fun at myself. I could have done a whole steamy shoot with half-naked male dancers, but I wanted to show my down-to-earth, fun side instead of always playing up to being a diva.

Instead, the video is a playful and funny montage of scenes in which I'm constantly taking selfies. The whole point was to make it comical rather than sexy.

The director, Paul Dadbridge, had never worked on a music video before. His background is short films, but when I saw the script for the scenes I was delighted and glad to be giving him his first shot at a music video.

We shot the footage in Bristol and the first scene of the day was in an industrial estate, at a car mechanic's. I was wearing a white low-cut vest top, little denim hotpants, overalls and black super-high heels.

'All the ladies in the club, let me see your hands up,' I sing while, erm, jacking a car up.

'Looking beautiful, got it going on, so stand up,' I continue, while distracting a mechanic with a porno 'tache and ponytail from his work, because… you know… I'm beautiful, obviously!

'Don't judge me, boy, don't judge me, boy, 'cause beauty ain't a crime,' I croon, as I'm sacked from my job at the garage for being too darn sexy and distracting.

The next scene of the day took place in a gym. Not one of your luxurious health-club type gyms, this was a spit-and-sawdust boxing place: rough, rugged and raw. I was dressed in a tiny sports bra showcasing my massive knockers, with tracksuit pants tight enough to leave nothing to the imagination.

In this clip I was boxing with another girl while D-Jukes was backing me in my corner. I loved filming this scene, and the girl I was supposedly punching was a good sport. I had to pretend to knock her out and then while I'm busy taking a selfie, she knocks me to the floor. It's one of the funniest moments in the whole video.

Just filming those two scenes took hours and hours. Truly exhausting, you wouldn't believe how much work goes into just a few seconds of footage. It took us so long we had to leave the rest of the scenes until the next day.

Last to shoot was the nightclub/party scene. For this I needed loads of extras for the shots so I invited everyone I knew: all my best friends, everyone on my Facebook. I even put a message out on Twitter, asking people from Bristol to be in my video.

Every single one of my mates told me they were going to come. So how many of them do you think actually turned up? Not one! I was gutted. This was my big moment and I wanted my real mates to be part of my video. I couldn't believe they all let me down like that. When I asked them where they were, they all had some excuse or said they forgot. Thank God for my loyal Twitter followers because at least forty of them turned up, which meant the scene could still go ahead. If they hadn't been there, I would have been left completely left in the lurch.

For this scene I was dressed in a form-fitting black leather jumpsuit. My hair was straight and parted to the side; my make-up was glamorous but not too overdone. This actually became the first scene you see on the finished video. I begin by strutting down some stairs, smiling and flicking my hair with attitude as I walk over to my rapper pal, D-Jukes.

I'm not going to lie, I was nervous with all these strangers around, watching my every move, but as soon as I got into the swing of things I absolutely worked it. I was determined to be strong, confident and driven to make this video the best that it could be. After all, everyone present had turned up for me, free of charge, to be in my video and that made me feel really good about myself.

A couple of weeks later when I saw the finished product, I was so made up I was literally screaming. I was like, 'Move over, Beyoncé, there's a new diva in town!' Suddenly it felt real. I was actually starring in my own music video with my own song. This was something I've wanted ever since I was old enough to speak, let alone sing. All credit to Paul and his skills as a director. We only had a limited budget of £3,000 and he managed to pull it off brilliantly; I couldn't have wished for anything better.

The video had its first play on MTV on 16 April 2014 and I got such a good reception from everyone who saw it. Everyone on Twitter was so complimentary and it felt great to get some praise for all the effort I'd put it. The single was then released on iTunes, peaking at number 36, which for a single with virtually no radio play is pretty damn impressive, if you ask me. My agent Luke told me all the radio stations snubbed my single because of my association with *The Valleys*, and I couldn't be taken seriously as a credible artist. Even MTV only played the video fourteen times on their own channels, which is better than nothing I suppose.

The whole experience was fantastic and it made me realise how much I actually do want to be part of the music industry. I've just been sent another song, which I'm hoping to record in spring 2015. An upbeat dance track, it's much more challenging than 'You Beautiful'. I'm hoping I can build on my first success and grow a bigger fan base.

Watch this space!

Chapter Twenty-five

THIRD TIME'S A CHARM

Take a look at the cast in Series One and then compare our appearance to that of Series Three. The difference was astonishing. I suppose it's the upside of a little notoriety – we were virtually able to make ourselves over free of charge. Many of us were constantly slated for our appearance and you wouldn't believe how much a stranger's nasty comment can affect you.

People used to constantly pick on me about my teeth on Twitter, so when Dr Rob from The Smile Clinic in Cardiff offered me discounted veneers in return for some publicity, I jumped at the chance. I would never have been able to afford a full set of gorgeous false pearly whites before the show, but now I had over 200,000 Twitter followers – I was a desirable advertisement.

I was also really unhappy with my boobs. All my life I'd been plagued by my massive nipples. The girls in the house used to say they were like burgers and it didn't half shatter my self-esteem. Luckily, my management, Misfits, had previously worked with an expert consultant plastic surgeon called Mr Miles Berry from Cosmetic Surgery Partners, who agreed to reduce my nipple size and give me free implants so long as I promoted his efforts in the press. My nipples had bothered me all my life and while I didn't want to share something that personal with the rest of the world, it was worth admitting to for the free surgery.

I used to get called 'bum chin' on Twitter, so the dimple was disguised with filler in my chin. Next up, my top lip was plumped out with Juvéderm to even out the pout. I also had a tiny bit of Botox in between my eyes to stop the 'elevens' crease forming.

It wasn't just me, either. Carley had new teeth. Nicole had new lips and new boobs. Jenna had even bigger breasts and AK had her choppers newly veneered after her first set of teeth were panned for being too horse-like. We were all cashing in on the free, plastic fantastic look, yet it was fuelled by the general public's harsh comments.

Sad, but true.

My breast surgery was filmed for Series Three and I was made up Nicole had come with me to hold my hand. Even though she didn't have to be there, she wanted to be because our friendship wasn't just for an audience, it went deeper than that. Which is why when we had a huge fight during this series, it completely devastated me... but we'll get to that part later.

Our first day of filming was always one of the best because we were all fresh and excited. Everyone was getting the party bus to the house, but I had other ideas. I loved the fact that I could play up to my diva queen image and I suggested that I could make my entrance on a huge grey horse while the others watched, like my peasants, from the side of the road. When they agreed, I was absolutely landed. I thought it was so funny and you know how I love to be the centre of attention. The scene was an absolute scream to film and one of the best I'd ever shot on the show.

Series Three came with a new addition too, a tattooed hunk

called Jack: part-time builder, part-time stripper, full-time piece of Welsh beefcake – apparently. When I first saw him I didn't fancy him, but the producers made it clear they wanted all the girls to flirt with him, which was fine by me because this was the first series where I didn't have a boyfriend.

I remember playing my single 'You Beautiful' and performing a sexy dance for Jack. He took it all in his stride and came back with the most lustful striptease. The lad had me on the floor, legs split like a kipper, grinding his tight cannonball ass into my crotch – it was a pretty horny moment. I knew then I was hot for Jack and I would make it my mission to have him on 'Teesha's leash throughout the series.

Now, let's discuss that huge fight between Nicole and me. For the most part it happened as you've seen it on screen but for those of you who can't remember, let me recap...

I was performing my single in Modo nightclub, Liverpool, and during the song Nicole and Jenna decided to take the shine off my performance by stripping on stage. The pair of them whipped out their tits, like a couple of backstreet lappies. So, were they trying to upstage me, or just pissed and not really thinking? Personally, I believe it was both, but it didn't really matter: the point was they had ruined my first-ever live performance and I was never going to get that opportunity back. Performing my single for a crowd had meant so much to me and now the whole experience was tarnished because of their stupid, slaggy behaviour. Maybe I would have expected that kind of carry-on from Jenna, but Nicole, my best friend in the world? She had truly upset me. And the worst part, she didn't even think she had done anything wrong.

We ended up crossing swords and I was happy to leave it until we had both sobered up, but Nicole wasn't. What hurt me even more was that she went straight over to Jenna and started slagging me off. To this day, I don't think I over-reacted and I was right to be tamping. I felt betrayed. Nicole was sniggering and laughing at me with Jenna, making jokes at my expense. It was like I was reliving those terrible school days when I was bullied by Cleo and Samantha. Worse than that, it felt like I was losing my best friend all over again.

All hell broke loose when Nicole and I started pushing each other. I couldn't believe we were going for each other and before I knew it, we were full-on fighting. I didn't think two girls with the kind of strong bond we had would ever be so vicious to one another. We scratched, punched, kicked and pulled each other's hair until eventually bouncers dragged us apart.

I felt terrible – I love Nicole and I never thought I'd fight with her. The whole situation was horrible and even though I've been through a lot of bad times in my life, this was one of the worst. It was like I'd been stabbed in the heart.

The producers were completely stunned by what had happened. They have a duty of care to look after each cast member, so it was decided I would have to stay elsewhere until we were back in Cardiff and could sort the matter out, soberly.

A few days later the female cast were summoned by the producers to sit down and watch the footage of the scrap. When I showed up, I couldn't even look at Nicole. Already, I was fighting back tears and witnessing the struggle on screen made me completely break down.

Although I didn't feel like the fight was my fault, I didn't walk away either so we were both in the wrong. Violence is never the answer and I'm ashamed we came to blows as we did. That was the first major row Nicole and I had. We both wept into each other's arms and apologised profusely. You could see how genuinely upset both of us were, and also how genuinely sorry we were. I hoped we were never going to argue like that again, but unfortunately it wasn't to be the end of our rocky relationship.

But for now, let's get back to Jack.

Despite me not really fancying him in the beginning, my feelings for Jack grew the more time we spent together. I suppose it's inevitable when you're living under the same roof. The first night I showed my interest was when I took him down to the cwtch. We ended up necking on with each other. He was a great kisser and after that, I began to look at him in a whole different light. It was then I started to get real feelings for him.

Maybe I should have told Jack how I felt, but I wanted to play it cool and let him chase me. I'll admit now I was upset when the next night he brought another girl back to the house. They were all over each other in front of me. I know we weren't an item, but if he ever wanted to be with me then he was going the wrong way about it.

The producers had seen how close we became, on and off camera. I'm not stupid, I know they were encouraging the romance between us, which is why they made Jack take me round to his mum's one afternoon. I knew it hadn't been his idea, but I still thought it was sweet of him to introduce me to her; he could have said no. When I saw how close Jack and his mum were, it made me melt a little bit and even though he wasn't my boyfriend, I wanted him to be.

Later the same day we had a party at the house. Stupidly, I thought because Jack and I had formed a bond, I wouldn't need to ask him not to get with other girls, but get on with another girl is exactly what he did. I should have realised then he wasn't interested in me. Instead I was tamping with the pair of them and ended up launching a pint of Coke in their direction. I was playing it real cool. Not!

I should have left it there with Jack, but when he begged my forgiveness I believed he was being genuine. And as the series went on, it looked like he wanted the same as me, to be more than just friends.

Jack was a proper gentleman and took me on a romantic dinner date, which meant a lot to me. In all my relationships I've never been wined and dined before. He was acting exactly like a boyfriend, but he still wasn't forthcoming with any kind of commitment. We were constantly kissing, holding hands and cwtching – it felt like we were really going to develop into something meaningful. I was so confused. Did he genuinely like me or was all this for the show?

But as one relationship was hotting up, another was going cold.

Nicole and I had drifted apart during this series. It had started with the fight, but when she began spending all her time with Jenna, I knew she had found a replacement for me. Nicole was still with Antony too, which always served as an underlying tension between us. Maybe she was jealous of my budding romance with Jack, and that's why they were always together, but it didn't stop me from feeling left out. And it wasn't long before we were embroiled in another booze-fuelled slanging match again. This time there was no punching or fighting, but the personal insults she threw hurt more than the time she'd slapped me. Much of our argument was cut from the show, but the part they left in was when she called me 'fat'. A best friend knows all your weaknesses and exactly how to hurt you.

When she said that I was really upset with her. Gutted, in fact. Imagine the worst things you think about yourself; not only does your best friend know about them too, she actually uses them in an argument against you in an attempt to ridicule you in front of the other housemates.

It took a while for us to patch things up after the row, but we did eventually apologise to each other. We couldn't take back what we'd said, we could only try and forget about it moving forwards.

By the end of the series I had really fallen for Jack and I thought we had something special. Queen Lateysha had finally found her king, I thought. I was really happy with him, happier than I'd been for years. He made so much effort buying me presents, flowers, chocolates, so forgive me for thinking we had something.

But I found out just after the series finished what had actually been going on.

I was keen to carry on the relationship away from the cameras, but as soon as we were back from Cardiff, Jack didn't want to know. His actions completely confused me and I just wanted to know where I stood with him.

A few days had gone by and Carley called me. She said that she'd had a conversation with Jack in which he basically admitted to just liking me in order to increase his own screen time and he didn't want to take things any further.

Now I'm not going to lie, I was gutted when she told me. I'd made myself vulnerable for him and he had totally made me look a fool. It's not cool to play with a girl's feelings for the sake of a TV show. I know I wasn't faking the way I felt and I couldn't believe he was. For this reason I have nothing more to do with Jack. I thought his behaviour was sly and underhand; I don't need people like that in my life.

I haven't really kept up to date with Jack's life since leaving the show, but I do know he went on to start a relationship with another girl, which is fine. Except that as soon as we finished filming, my agent Luke (who was also Jack's agent) had filled both our schedules with work comprised of a lot of nightclub PAs (personal appearances) in the hope of Jack and I being together. Awkward wasn't the word!

It didn't help that on most of the club PAs Jack brought his new girlfriend, too. Although she and I quickly dismissed any tensions with a hug and a kiss and a chat over a vodka, it was always difficult. I just got on with my job and tried to be professional. To be fair, so did Jack. That said, the club PAs after Series Three weren't the same as those before it, and all too often Luke would be on the phone to me, having a go. Apparently the club managers were always moaning that Jack and I sat in different corners of the room.

With Nicole, things are OK now, but we're nowhere near as close as we once were. Since the show, she has spent a lot of time working in Magaluf – she seems to really enjoy it. We do speak every now and then on WhatsApp or FaceTime, but again, our friendship is a shadow of its former self, but that's now true for me with everyone from the show.

Chapter Twenty-six

TWITTER WAR

I don't even want to pay any lip service to that gravel-voiced, *TOWIE* tit-head James Lock, but since our Twitter spat made the national press and I have never really had my chance to speak about why it happened, it's time to set the record straight. And unlike his show's pretend drama, this all happened for real.

Natalee, James and myself had been booked on a PA at De Montfort University Student Union in Leicester one evening on 2 October 2013. It was billed as a *TOWIE* vs. *The Valleys* night. Students could come, chat and have their photos taken with us.

We originally met James in the hotel before we were due to travel to the venue. He was staying in the room next door to us and when we first greeted each other, I remember him making some lame joke about having a little pyjama party with us afterwards. You should be so lucky, James! I think it's best to mention here that James at this point had a girlfriend – a lovely-looking girl called Danielle Armstrong, who also featured on *TOWIE*.

James had invited a couple of his friends with him on the PA and they seemed like a good bunch to Natalee and me. After a few introductions, we all travelled down to the club together in a minibus taxi and at first I thought James seemed like a really nice guy. He was polite, chatty and up for a good night, just what you need on a PA.

As the evening progressed, my opinion of James only got better. He was pouring our drinks, making us laugh, dancing and flirting like mad with us. Natalee had a boyfriend and didn't really give him the time of day, but I was just laughing at all his stupid chat-up lines. He would come over to me, put his hand around my waist and whisper in my ear, 'I bet you're a devil in bed!' I'll admit he made me a little bashful. He has this charm about him. He'd continue by saying, 'How big are your boobs? Are you going to show them to me later?' I just kind of rolled my eyes towards the ceiling because I didn't know how to react.

As the night progressed, he continued to get a lot more hands-on with both Natalee and me. I remember I had to stop him and ask him outright, 'Haven't you got a girlfriend?' and his response shocked me.

'No,' he laughed. 'I'm only with Danielle for the show. If I wasn't with her, I would have no storylines. I don't even like her, I don't even fancy her.'

I was completely stunned.

'So, is the show scripted?' I asked.

'Yeah, the show is completely scripted,' James replied. 'I barely knew Danielle. I was forced to go out with her by the producers.'

'Really? They just told you to date her?'

'They had a few girls in mind, but out of them all I picked Danielle because she had the best tits!' he laughed. 'Although, they aren't as nice as yours.'

Now, I don't know if what James was telling me was the truth, or he was saying it just because he wanted to get into me, but either way that's a million per cent what he said to me.

We stayed at the club for about three hours and it's fair to say we were all suitably wrecked. We wanted to leave the student union but it was too early to go back to the hotel, which is when James had the bright idea of taking Natalee and me to a strip club. Most girls would have said no, but I was buzzing – I love strip clubs!

As soon as we got in there, we looked around at the strippers and they were absolutely hanging! I remember they were all jealous of Natalee and me being with James. After eyeing up every single one of the ladies, we settled on a girl with long blonde hair – quite skinny, with a big tattoo on her thigh. She gave each and every one of us a dance. James's rich pal was footing the bill otherwise I would have never bothered with a dance because the girl was terrible.

I've always been attracted to stripping and I knew I could do better, so I got up and gave everyone a striptease in the club. Everyone was appreciative of my moves and they laughed and cheered as I spun myself round the pole. Eventually, we decided to go back to the hotel and even though Natalee and me were absolutely shattered by this point, James wanted to carry on the party.

The tango-coloured tool had whipped off his top and kept banging on our door, begging (and I *do* mean begging) us for a threesome. But the pair of us just laughed at him. He was standing there, with his naked torso pressed up against the door, pleading with us to let him in. Sadly for him, neither of us was interested.

The next day, he followed us both on Twitter and we agreed we would have to do it again some time. We had all had a laugh and despite his obvious advances, we thought he was cool. It was actually one of the better PAs I'd ever been on.

All was well for a while but trust that perma-tanned toad to stick the knife in.

It was a couple of months later when Carley called me to say she had read an article quoting James Lock slagging us off.

He'd said in a piece with the *Gay Times* magazine: 'With something like *The Valleys*, the public are laughing at them, not with them. And *Geordie Shore* is very seedy. It's just a house full of idiots being videotaped and getting pissed.

'*The Valleys* is an absolute joke. The thing is, you meet them and think they won't be as bad in real life. But I've met a couple of the girls and they really are that bad.

'I don't mean this in a snobby way, but they're just not the sort of people you want to associate with. Going out and having a laugh is one thing but it's another thing going out and being disrespectful.'

When I read what he'd said I was furious. He wasn't saying we were that bad when he was trying to shag the pair of us behind his girlfriend's back, was he? What a joke!

I couldn't hold back, so I took to Twitter to vent my feelings towards him and let everyone know what a scumbag he really is.

I wrote: 'Hahahaha @JamesLockie86 are you actually serious calling Geordie Shore and The Valleys idiots! How f**king rude ... So cheeky!

'So much I could say right now but keeping my mouth shut. Lol. Cheat.

'Quite sad when people have to slag other people off for publicity lol. #sleeze #youreacheat.

'At least our show isn't scripted and we don't have to "get" with each other for storylines like you told me on that PA @ JamesLockie86'.

He replied with: '@LateyshaValleys Winge winge winge!! F**k off you old stinka!'

So I said: '@JamesLockie86 your such a Sleeze ball it's funny! Remember the strip club when you had a gf? Yeah thought so. And I'm 21 babe!'

He ended his pathetic tirade with: '@LateyshaValleys hahahaha....don't even go there! I know a couple of geezas that wanna know your name! F**k off now your boring me!!

'@LateyshaValleys and as for the 21!! F**k me did u have an up hill paper round!? #roughlife.'

It's fair to say, there's no love lost between us. He is an absolute dirty pig and does exactly the same thing as *The Valleys* and the *Geordie Shore* lads do, but his actions just aren't filmed in the same way. In fact, he's far worse because he's not even honest about it. If he thought we were that bad and disgusting, why was he practically breaking down our hotel room door? He's such a lying hypocrite. The thing was we actually got along with him on the night. We'd had such a good time I couldn't understand why he would say it in the first place.

After about twenty minutes James took all his tweets down because people were messaging him, saying it's disgusting how he speaks to women. This all happened around the same time as he had a row with co-star Gemma Collins from *TOWIE*, where he was making fun of her looks and weight.

Just after our Twitter row Gemma actually tweeted me a private supportive message, which was nice of her. I suppose we had something in common. James is such a cruel bastard, I don't know who he thinks he is.

Anyway, that's the God's honest truth about what happened. I'm fully expecting James to call me a liar, but Natalee will back me up. We know who's got form for lying here and it certainly isn't me.

Chapter Twenty-seven

PARISIAN DREAM

My current boyfriend is a complete sweetheart and very different from all the other guys I've been out with. His name is Ben, and even though I have known him for about six years, we didn't actually meet until December 2013.

We connected on Facebook back in 2008, when I was with Ryan. He liked one of my photos and then I liked one of his in return. It seems so silly saying this out loud, but that's the truth. I've always thought he was a good-looking guy, completely my type: mixed race, tall, cool dresser, absolutely stunning smile and wicked personality. He also has a gorgeous body – super-athletic, toned, and with an envious six-pack most men can only dream of.

When I first met him he was playing football for Reading, but the club released him due to a bad injury. These days, he's a successful personal trainer and kids' football coach. I love that side to him. It's so nice to see him interact with children and he's great with them too. I didn't know I looked for those qualities in a man, but it's nice when your guy encompasses it all.

When we first added each other on Facebook we would chat now and again. Every time we always planned to meet up, but for whatever reason it never happened. Either I had a boyfriend or he had a girlfriend, and it just never seemed to be the right time for us. Sometimes we would go months without speaking to each other. Other times, we would be in regular contact.

Just after I'd finished Series Three of *The Valleys*, I was feeling pretty low about the whole Jack thing. Maybe Ben knew instinctively because after months of not speaking, he sent me a text message out of the blue. It was nothing to read into, he was just asking me how it was going. I smiled when I saw it. I'd always thought Ben was a sweet guy and I was glad to have heard from him again.

After that we began messaging regularly about all kinds of stuff and I found him really easy to open up to – he was a good listener and I felt like I could tell him anything without being judged. Soon we were messaging each other all day, every day. Every night we would be on the phone for three hours at a time and even though we had never met before physically, I felt like we knew each other inside out.

During one of our marathon chats, he asked me what I was doing for New Year and I had zero plans. Then he said, 'Would you like to go to Paris?' It's every girl's dream to be invited to Paris with a guy you really like, isn't it? Nice things like that never happen to girls like me and so I was over the moon when he asked me.

Although it sounds weird, going abroad with a man you have never actually met, I was pretty sure he was a good guy and I knew I would have a laugh with him, if nothing else. We each paid for our tickets and that was that: our first date was finally set.

Two days before New Year I jumped on a coach to London,

which took forever but it gave me a chance to do my make-up and make myself look stunning for Ben. I really wanted to make a good impression. What girl wouldn't?

The first time I clapped eyes on him was when he joined the bus journey in London before it continued to Dover. I was so nervous and he was even better looking in real-life than in his pictures; I was instantly smitten. After we got the initial awkwardness out of the way, we grew comfortable really quickly and I felt like we'd known each other forever.

Flights were extortionate at that time of year, so to cut down on costs we took the ferry over to Calais and then got on another bus to Paris. It was a really long-winded way to travel but we wanted to spend the majority of our money on doing things in the French capital, not wasting it on getting there.

We spent three nights in Paris and one of the evenings we went to Disneyland to watch the world-famous firework display, which is still to this day one of the most magical moments of my life. I've seen firework displays before, but nothing quite like this. As a little girl, I had longed to go to Disneyland, but I was never going to get the chance with a family like mine. So, to be there at the magic kingdom, staring up at Sleeping Beauty's castle, watching the most incredible display of fireworks and listening to 'When You Wish Upon a Star' made me feel truly happy; it was a fantasy come true.

The whole night was absolutely incredible and at the end of it, Ben took my hand in his, looked deep into my eyes and – like the romantic he is – asked me to be his girlfriend. What did the Walt Disney song say? Someday my prince will come? Well, mine came all right – right there, under the magic of the pink castle. I instantly said yes, because it felt right and you'll be pleased to know we have been living happily ever after ever since.

However life isn't always fairy tales and sometimes it can be difficult because Ben lives in London and I live in Wales, but we make it work. I remember when I finished with Ryan, I never, ever thought I would meet someone and be able to love him like I did Ryan. But when I met Ben, he made me realise that I love him even more. And it doesn't matter how many celebrities I meet or how many men try it on with me, I feel with Ben I have something really special and I would never want to mess it up. I'm so grateful to him for everything that he is, for the way he makes me feel and for loving me in the way that he does.

He is such a nice person and more importantly, he lets me be who I want to be, which is always important in a relationship. He never tells me I can or can't do anything; he's so relaxed and cool in that way.

When I told him I'd planned a trip to Miami for six weeks with my girls, he didn't bat an eyelid. Of course he was gutted he was going to miss me, but he never once said, you are not going or attempted to stop me, unlike many of my mates' boyfriends. He knows I need to make the most of my younger years and I would only have resented him if he hadn't let me go.

I know I'm young but I see my entire future with Ben. I can't ever imagine loving anyone else in the same way, nor do I want to. I think I've found the one.

No relationship is perfect, least of all ours. Yeah, we argue and shout at each other at times, but the foundations are rock solid. I'm more inclined to want to work through problems than create unnecessary ones and give up when times get a little tough.

I know I shouldn't keep comparing the two relationships, but when I was with Ryan I would sometimes ask myself, 'Is he the one?' 'Do I feel the way I should about him?' or 'Is this relationship going well?' I realised my doubts answered my own question.

When you're not sure whether you're in love with someone or not, the answer is almost certainly not.

Never have I looked at a man and been so in love before. I want Ben to be the father of my children and if it happened anytime soon, I would be overjoyed.

I could have written this whole book on how incredible my boyfriend is, but one, that would be really boring for you guys, and two, I kind of want to keep what we have private. So much of my life has been out there for all to see and comment on, I prefer to keep this piece for myself. All you need to know is he is wonderful in every way.

I want to kiss him, and only him, for the rest of our lives.

Chapter Twenty-eight

LOVE SASHA

It's always been an ambition of mine to have my own clothing range. I'd been offered a few during my time on *The Valleys,* but for a number of reasons they never seemed right, or I just wasn't blown away by the clothes or the style of the company. That was until I came across Love Sasha and I don't know, I suppose I just got a good feeling about the business.

The guy who owns the brand, Mike Murray, is great and we have built up a fantastic professional relationship. He's twenty-one and really easy to get on with. I love his ambition and I know he will go on to be a huge success in the future. It really is a joy to work with him.

I'll be honest, though, at first I think he was dubious about having me promote his brand. *The Valleys* girls aren't known for their high-fashion sense, are they? Plus, our antics on screen can put off potential companies. But after a few meetings and a photo shoot, we agreed a trial run to see how sales would go after I helped promote their items.

I chose Love Sasha because I wanted a range that was affordable for young girls. When I was growing up, I had no money to spend on expensive clothes, so I didn't want the items to be too pricey. The range starts at the crazy low price of £3.99 and the most expensive item is £39.99. The main qualities I was looking for in the brand were it had to be young, funky, affordable, current and disposable.

I'm not one of those girls who will just put my name to a range, either. From the beginning I made it clear that I wanted to have some say; and I have a very large input over the items I wish to include. Mike was pleased when I said I wanted to be involved and invited me down to the warehouse to handpick the stock. I thought the warehouse was going to be this big glamorous building, but it was this old derelict place in the middle of an industrial estate in Manchester. It was quite late in the evening when I arrived, it was dark and I honestly thought I'd been lured there and something terrible was about to happen, although when I went inside it was like the most amazing Aladdin's cave of clothes. There was rack upon rack of garments; I really was spoilt for choice.

My initial contract was small. It was agreed that if Love Sasha sold more than £1,500 worth of my stock in the first month, they would renew my contract for a longer period. When the clothing line launched and they totted up the sales figures, astonishingly they'd sold over £9,000, which was absolutely out of this world! The company were so impressed with the sales and I was delighted to have made it into a success.

Naturally, after they looked at the numbers, they immediately asked me to renew my contract, and ever since the sales are growing month on month. I make it all sound so easy, don't I? But starting a new clothing range is anything but. Some of the other *Valleys* girls have tried to follow suit with their own ranges and have failed.

Nicole and Jenna's agent set one up for them and, strangely, they never told me about it. The funny thing was, the day I found out I had been with them in London and they didn't say a word. It was Mike from Love Sasha who told me later that night. I sent them a text, saying, 'Are you doing a clothing range, too?' They both replied with something along the lines of, 'Yeah, well, the details haven't been worked out yet. We were going to tell you.'

But that's what I mean, when I say we are all so competitive. It's like no one wants anyone to do well, and it really is a shame. Anyway, I didn't care – I already had my clothing line well established – but I was just a little annoyed that I had to find out from Mike and not from my so-called best friends. I wished them well with it because I'm not bitter.

Since its launch in 2013, my range has gone from strength to strength. I could live off the income I get from Love Sasha alone, because it's becoming that successful. Sometimes I have to pinch myself because I remember when I had virtually no money and had to live off my boyfriend Ryan. When I was growing up, my family could never afford new clothes for me. It was for this reason that I had a brainwave one evening. I called Mike and asked him if he would be willing to do a 49p sale for a couple of hours. He immediately thought I was crazy, but I wanted to give back to the girls who were as poor as me, back in the day.

Despite Mike thinking I was deranged, he agreed to go along with it and understood my reasoning. I was adamant it would work, so I tweeted from my account, saying some of the dresses were now at the bargain low price of 49p. People were gobsmacked. They accused me of running a scam, but it was 100 per cent genuine.

The items sold out in literally minutes and so many customers were accessing the site that it eventually crashed.

Don't get me wrong, we lost loads of money because we were selling at lower than cost price, but it was a promotional offer. The range had been doing so well in all the other months we'd been selling, we could afford to take the hit. And the plan worked well. Everyone was talking about the brand and the clothes, which was the goal from the start: brand awareness. Plus, Love Sasha gained loads of new followers on Twitter and many more repeat customers every month.

People thought I was being ridiculous when I'd come up with that plan. All the other girls on the show were a bit snotty, saying the clothes were too cheap and that's why they had to be sold at that price. I'll agree it was a risky tactic, but in the end it all worked out for the best. I'd a gut feeling it would work and I just had to trust my instincts. I let everyone say what he or she wanted, but at the end of the day, it's me laughing all the way to the bank every month.

My family were really proud of me and my mum is pleased with how well I'm doing. She never really got to have much of a youth because she had me so young, so I think she kind of lives her life vicariously through me now, which is nice. I've treated my nearest and dearest to some of the best items from my clothing range and they are always so appreciative. It's great that I can now treat my friends and family in the ways that I do because they've always been there for me through everything.

Chapter Twenty-nine

RUMOUR
HAS IT

The Valleys Series Three aired in February 2014 and we had really strong viewing figures. I won't lie, they did dip slightly as the series went on, but we opened with big audiences and everyone was pleased with the overall reception. Usually, if viewing figures are bad, everyone starts panicking and the channel will look for people to blame. Like production, marketing, press and so on, but our channel wasn't so we were blissfully unaware of what was about to happen.

The viewing figures for our show came through a week later. They are a combination of how many viewers watch live, on plus one and online.

I'm well aware that this is going to sound like I'm a big-headed brat, but I had provided much of the content for Series Three. Without me shaking things up, it would never have been as good as it was. With this in mind, I asked Luke, my manager, if he would negotiate a pay rise and to be honest, he thought the same and encouraged me to think that way. The notion that making

The Valleys Series Four was in question just wasn't on the cards. No one expected it to be axed when it did, least of all me.

While the series was on there were loads of adverts for MTV's new reality show, *Ex on the Beach*, because it started the Tuesday after our show finished. That week, Luke had a meeting with Manus and Fiona from True North, the production company who made *The Valleys*. He went to discuss a pay rise with them – quite a big one too. I was asking for a big pay increase for Series Four. Even though the production budget was tight and we were under the impression that there would be no cast pay rise, Luke was willing to go against that and ask for more money on my behalf. Essentially, I would have been paid double the rest of the cast.

Although it was a big ask, if you don't ask, you don't get (as you know). It wasn't an outrageous ask, either – I gave so much to that show, more than the others in my opinion. Anyway, even if I didn't get more money, I was kind of hoping that the discussion would lead to all of us getting a bigger fee, not just me. That's the truth.

It was after that meeting that Luke first told me he had concerns for the future of *The Valleys*. An email came round with the *Ex on the Beach* viewing figures. Unfortunately for the rest of the *Valleys* cast and me, they were really, really good.

They had achieved the highest average audience among 16–34s for a launch episode of a new series in the channel's history. I don't wish to bore you with figures, but the launch show attracted an average audience of 328,000 – 34 per cent higher than the launch of *Geordie Shore* in 2011, and 73 per cent higher than *The Valleys* in 2012. So, as you can see, they were extremely good.

I guess it also comes with less drama because it doesn't have a permanent cast. They are in and out after one series so production don't have to deal with egos and there's no huge green screen filming period afterwards, which I imagine is so very expensive.

When Luke relayed the news to me, I kept thinking, why the hell wouldn't there be a Series Four? We were becoming more liked and better known; all we needed now was a little while longer to become more established. I suspected that our show cost more and that I wanted to be paid more, but they had invested so much, why quit now?

Still, we all hoped they would commission a fourth series and sign off on the budgets. Manus and Fiona were worried too because everyone had worked so hard on the series, including themselves and Steve at *MTV*. When I heard all this, I was heartbroken. Finally, I had found something in my life that worked for me and it looked like it would be snatched away; it was all out of my control, too.

At this point I didn't relay my fears to the other cast members, I just wanted to keep it to myself and hope nothing would come of it.

Then I remember getting the call from Luke. It was about 9am and he sounded really sad on the phone. I knew before he even told me that it was going to be bad news and when he finally confirmed my worst fears, I felt sick. Although I felt deflated, at least I had been kind of prepared. I always knew *The Valleys* would end one day but I never expected it to be after just three series. I'd hoped we might emulate the success of *Geordie Shore*, which is now on to its tenth series. I always thought I would be the one to leave the show rather than the show leaving me.

Although I was absolutely gutted, I still had work coming in thick and fast. I had my clothing line, glamour shoots, personal appearances and my sponsored tweets. I was earning OK money, not amazing, but I was getting a decent amount for what I was putting in and way more than anyone else on *The Valleys*. I knew I would have to curb my spending and make everything last as long as possible because now I was back to square one and I didn't know where my next pay cheque was coming from.

All the cast were told on the same day and we were equally gutted. We had given up our lives, including our jobs and relationships, to be part of the show and now we were left with nothing. Some of them took the news worse than others. Jenna was crying her eyes out daily because she had a mortgage to pay. Chidgey was also devastated – he thought he was made for life. Meanwhile, Carley had had enough of the show anyway and took it in her stride.

I felt completely embarrassed, like it was our fault. Maybe we hadn't performed the way we should, or could have done things differently. I was so ashamed, I couldn't tell anyone. The only people I spoke to were the cast and we all agreed to stay quiet about the axing of the show, so we could make as much money as possible while we could.

It was only when I was on a trip to Ibiza in June 2014 on a research mission to write this book that I got a message from the girls in the cast, telling me the news had been leaked to *Heat* magazine. I don't know how they knew, but I suppose bad news travels fast and soon MTV confirmed to the world that *The Valleys* was no more.

Now, I would have to tell everyone. I hadn't even told my best friend Harrison, my boyfriend Ben, or even my mum. I suppose I just wanted to digest the news on my own, without everyone's questions or pity. The thing I was most angry about was that while there were no rumours about the show being axed, we all got steady work. Now the cat was out of the bag, clients began to find out and in turn the work started to dwindle. In fact, it pretty much stopped. Everyone around me was so supportive. I didn't know what I was going to do next but I remember my mum sitting me down at the kitchen table and telling me how proud she was of me. It was a truly special moment, especially because they had been so rare over the years. I think she always assumed I knew she was proud of me, but it was amazing to have her tell me.

Luckily, from the point I had learned that the show was in jeopardy, I had begun saving and drastically slowed my spending down. I was due to buy a new MacBook laptop, but without knowing where my next pay cheque was coming from, I didn't.

For the first time since I began *The Valleys*, I started being sensible with my cash. Let me tell you, it was a nasty feeling; I felt sick to the pit of my stomach. Now, I had no stability, no investments, and nothing to fall back on.

My life, as I knew it, was officially over.

Chapter Thirty

ARE YOU SERIOUS?

At first I thought all was lost and the nation would never be able to see my unsightly mug on TV again, but after much hard work, my manager Luke bagged me my very own TV show, aptly titled *Are You Serious?* because I say those three words constantly.

The show is a mix of *Rude Tube*, *Harry Hill's TV Burp* and *You've Been Framed*. It's featured on a Sky music channel called Planet Pop. I know all the other *Valleys* cast members were insanely jealous, but the break hadn't come easy for me.

First of all, I sat down with a team of comedic writers to hash out a script. Next, I shot a pilot show – which was all funded by my agent – and took a good while to film, mainly because I'd lost my voice! Not good when the majority of what I had to do was talk all the way through it. I'd love to tell you I lost my voice through being genuinely ill, but let's be honest, it's because I'd been out till all hours, getting smashed. Naturally, the crew and my agent were fuming. I did feel guilty, but how the hell did

I know I was going to lose my voice? Usually, I can power on through a hangover, but laryngitis can't be covered up so easily with concealer.

The pilot was shown to a few channels and, luckily, Planet Pop really liked it (they had been looking for a show of this type for some time). Although they weren't very happy about my lack of vocal chords, they decided to give me a small budget to film another episode.

The only time I had to squeeze in more filming was just before I was due to go on holiday to Miami and after a PA in the Netherlands. I was instructed to do the PA, stay sober and then catch a flight back to the UK into Liverpool to crack on with filming. Sounds pretty simple, doesn't it?

You would have thought I might have learnt my lesson after the first pilot disaster, but I don't know, when I'm out and I get the taste for a couple of drinks, I find it hard to stop. Luke had already read me the riot act and warned me not to start boozing in the club in the Netherlands, but I thought he was being too harsh. In the end he agreed I could limit myself to four drinks as long as I got plenty of sleep and left the club at 2am – as per the agreement.

Like an overbearing dad, he was constantly messaging me all the way through the night to make sure I wasn't getting hammered. But I messed up royally when I started sending snapchats. He saw there was a table of Jagerbombs in one snapchat and then an empty table of Jagerbomb glasses in the next. I wish I could have said that's all I drank, but stupidly, I was necking anything put in front of me. Vodka? Yep! Wine? Yep! Shots? Plenty!

Eventually, I left the club when the DJ turned the lights on at 5am and that was only because the place was closing! I was absolutely slaughtered when I left and to this day, I couldn't tell you how I got back to my hotel room – I just remember getting back there and collapsing on the bed. My original plan was to pack my stuff and get to the airport ready for my flight at 8am, but because I was completely wasted, I missed the luxury British Airways flight.

You can imagine how furious Luke was with me and I was devastated when the next flight he organised was on Ryanair, an hour later. Now, I'm not being a diva, but I always get hassled on those flights by rowdy stag and hen dos. I was certainly not in the mood for photos and people that morning; all I desperately craved was some sleep.

I've never felt so bad in all my life, literally the hangover from hell. My head hurt like someone was pounding nine-inch nails into the back of my skull. I remember being on the flight, sunglasses firmly in place, with the weight of my forearm on my forehead. Shivering, all I could do was try not to be sick.

Luke was picking me up from Liverpool's John Lennon Airport and as I went through passport control, he asked me, 'Would you prefer a coffee, Red Bull and McDonald's or a bottle of vodka?' I think he was trying to be sarcastic but maybe the vodka wasn't such a bad idea. Even though the idea of alcohol turned my stomach, I thought maybe if I stayed pissed I could quite easily carry on through the day's filming. In the end I did the sensible thing and chose food and coffee. One sniff of Russia's finest and I would almost certainly have hurled!

As soon as I got in the car, I was given a lecture like you wouldn't believe. I know it was wrong to get so hammered, but I just couldn't help myself. As far as I was concerned, I was on a PA in a different country without any friendly faces around me so I needed to be lubricated to have a good time. I hate doing things on my own. Would you believe I feel self-conscious at times? Copious amounts of alcohol make me lose my inhibitions, which, by the way, is not the best way to build your confidence, but it's the only way I know.

Even after the food I still felt close to death, but Luke was relentless. He had no sympathy and dragged me off to the TV studios after my last gulp of coffee. We filmed the pilot at a place called Toxeth TV in Liverpool. When I first arrived and saw the street – Windsor Street – I remember thinking, *Why the fuck has he brought me here?* The area surrounding the studios was horrid and if I could have bolted right then and there, I would have done so. To be fair, the studios inside were nice and the crew were all pretty friendly when I walked in.

I'm not joking, that hangover was up there with the best of them! The whole day was horrendous. I was sat having my make-up done, trying my utmost not to barf all over the poor make-up artist. The hairdresser kept pulling on my extensions to blow them, which made my head pound even more. Honestly, I can't begin to explain the world of pain I was in. I'd never had a hangover quite like it – it must have been that cheap foreign ale I wasn't used to.

For the pilot, I had to do about 800 takes of links and sections. I kept messing up my first few attempts, which is why it was taking so long. Every time I delivered a line, they would say, 'More energy!' or 'Do it again without slurring this time!' Not only this, they wanted me to dance about, twerk, toss my hair and shake my booty. It was beyond exhausting.

To put it mildly, I was hanging out of my arsehole!

It's a good job the director John Owens was a great guy, who was so patient with me – he must be a saint. The comedy writer Eddie Fortune was also a star and had me in stitches all day. They both helped to keep my spirits up when I needed them most. High-five to the pair of them!

By the end of the day I had done four outfit changes, filmed about seventy links, the promo and some fillers sections. And it had taken ten hours in total! When the crew finally shouted, 'That's a wrap!' I was absolutely thrilled. In fact, I was deliriously happy!

Unbelievably, I didn't want to waste my stunning hair and make-up, so when a few of my Liverpool pals messaged me to go out in the city, I thought about it for a whole ten seconds before replying, 'Of course'. I'd found a second wind from somewhere and ended up out on the lash again that night. I must have been running on adrenalin or something, I don't know where I found the energy. The whole time I was stifling yawns, but still, I hadn't seen my mates in ages and wasn't about to waste my gorgeous look sitting on a train back to Port Talbot. You know what they say: you can sleep when you're dead.

Luckily, when it was all edited together, the channel loved the promo. Can you imagine if they hadn't after all that messing around? I would have been tamping! Delighted with what we'd shot and the whole concept for the show, they signed an exclusive deal with me. The show is due to air in the spring of 2015 and I can't wait for you all to see it.

I can't believe I pulled it off in the end. Presenting is something I've wanted to get into for a while and finally, I was given my chance thanks to my amazing manager Luke. It's a step away from *The Valleys* and a step towards trying to establish myself as Lateysha Grace, who hopefully will be a credit-worthy presenter for many years to come.

Chapter Thirty-one

WELCOME TO MIAMI

Someone once told me, 'Almost everything strange washes up near Miami'. And they're not wrong. The city is like a neon jungle Barbie world. Everything is pink, plastic, and there are luscious palm trees everywhere.

Everyone goes up and down Ocean Drive in exotic cars, posing in crazy sunglasses, usually on their way to some backstreet alley warehouse, where you'll find a sick party. People-watching is my favourite pastime – you see all kinds of weird and wonderful sorts rattling up and down the street. I say 'rattling' because literally everyone is on some kind of drug, legal or not. At least, that was my first impression when I got to Miami and for the whole six weeks I was there, strange became the norm.

Take our first night out, for example. I say 'our' because in September 2014, I had travelled to Miami with some girls I knew from Wales: Erin, Nina and Armi. We had decided to take a massive six-week holiday there and ever since then I'd been working my ass off to be able to afford it. We didn't want to arrive and have to scrimp on anything.

The first time we all went out, we hit a club called Dream, in the heart of South Beach. There were two levels to the club – a dance floor and a mezzanine – which is where all the famous faces were sitting when we arrived. That particular night, a guy called Snootie Wild – an up-and-coming rapper in America – came in with his entourage and took the upper level so everyone in the club could get a good look at him. Within minutes, he had spotted me and waved me up to his table. Out of all the girls in the club, he had his eye on *me*! I was squealing with delight on the inside, like really flattered. Obviously, I had my boyfriend Ben at home, so I wasn't ever going to do anything with this guy, but I was just fully gasping to have been invited to sit with him.

He was with about ten other guys, all dressed up to the nines in garish Gucci trainers and Louis Vuitton monogram hoodies. They were draped in so much bling they could have given Mr. T a run for his money – tacky, right?

A little while after we had met them, Snootie asked my friends and me to go back to a party. I wasn't particularly keen, especially after that crazy incident in London all those years before, but my friend Erin persuaded me it would be fine. I'll admit then I began to get excited. This was my first night out in Miami, already I'd been called over to a famous rapper's table and now we were being invited back to party with him! I was acting really cool, like these things happened all the time, but still I couldn't quite believe it.

We walked outside the club, over to their cars and my jaw literally dropped. In front of us stood a white Porsche, a white Ferrari, a white Range Rover, a white Maserati and a red Lamborghini. These guys had some serious cash!

The other girls went home, but Erin and me jumped into the Range Rover, with Snootie and his mate Paul, who was driving. I remember being in the back of the car and almost wanting to cry with happiness. Things like this didn't happen to a *Valleys* reject like me! I was from a scummy place in Port Talbot and now I was in Miami, being driven in a top-class Range Rover, back to a house for a cool party with a rapper. It was beyond my wildest dreams.

Pulling up to the house, I was literally gobsmacked. The place was like the mansion you see on *Keeping Up With The Kardashians*. Absolutely huge, it had its own private gates, long, sweeping gardens, a pond full of Koi carp and there was a massive, kidney-shaped swimming pool. It was incredible! I'd never seen a house more beautiful in all my life and I couldn't believe our driver, Paul, was the owner. I mean he looked like he had money, but not *that* kind of money.

The party was amazing! Tons of guys and girls turned up, every room seemed to be packed with people. In the living room, Paul told us there was a pole we could have a go on and since both Erin and myself had had pole-dancing lessons in the past, we decided to show the crowd what we were made of.

I wrapped one leg around the cold, steel rod, spinning my body round at the same time. Then I tossed my hair over my shoulders and slid my backside down the pole before I came to a squat position. Thrusting my legs open, I got my first cheer as the party got a look at my crotch. It was the kind of feedback I needed at the time and gave me an added boost to carry on. I decided to attempt a more complicated move I'd learned, and I just hoped my strength and thighs wouldn't let me down now.

Cradling your body round a pole takes immense upper body strength and a lot of concentration. If you misjudge the height of your hands, you will most likely fall like a fairy elephant to the floor. I had to judge my move just right. *Well, here goes nothing*, I thought. Placing my hands above my head, I made a big leap towards the pole, letting my leg encircle the steel and the momentum drift me round. The pros call this the 'hook and roll' and I'd nailed it! I was so happy; the adrenalin was pumping through my body. I was thrilled I'd executed the move to plan and I loved the feeling of power it gave me. Another cheer ensued from the party and I couldn't help but smile. The crowd were uniformly appreciative and began throwing dollars at Erin and me. It was all good fun and who knows, if I practised hard enough, I might be able to be a professional pole dancer one day.

I didn't half get a thrill from it!

About a week after we partied with Snootie, I met a really cool guy called Prince on the beach one afternoon. Bold as brass, he came over and introduced himself to us. His confidence was unwavering and we ended up hanging with him for a couple of hours. We learned that this dazzle-smiled black hotty was self-titled 'Prince' because he was apparently the 'Fresh Prince of Miami'. He knew everyone and everything about the city. A promoter for the hottest clubs, he was a guy worth knowing.

That evening he invited us out to Cameo club in downtown Miami, where he said he would kindly let us – Erin, Nina and me – use his table, so we could dance, party and have somewhere to throw our bags. We would never have been able to afford a table ourselves because even the most basic came with a $3,000 minimum spend.

The night was pretty tame – well, by Miami's standards, anyway – but it was about to get a whole lot wilder when I looked over to my right and thought I saw one of the world's most famous rappers walk in. At first, I thought I must be mistaken but when he and his entourage sat down on a table just yards away from ours, I got a better view and realised it was, in fact, the man I thought it was – Drake.

For those of you who don't know, Drake is one of the hottest, if not *the* hottest, rapper in the world right now. His discography goes on for miles. Not only that but he is the man behind most current R 'n' B mega-hits.

My stomach instantly flipped. I remember going to see him at a concert in Manchester, but there he was, in the flesh, sitting just three feet away from me. I was literally hyperventilating at the thought of being in the same room. Without further ado, I grabbed Erin and Nina, and rushed them to the bathroom so we could assess our look. I had to know I was looking fly before I could even begin to cast a glance in his direction.

We reapplied our lip gloss, fluffed our hair and powdered on more blusher. Then, as we always did, we did a 360-degree spin inspection on each other to make sure there was nothing out of place. Satisfied we looked as good as possible, we strutted back out to the club. We must have looked like three fierce bitches, walking back in with our newfound confidence. Plenty of guys had been copping an eyeful of us and they were all vying for our attention, but we only had eyes for Drake.

We sat back down with Prince at his table and within twenty minutes of overtly flirting in Drake's direction, one of his minders approached us.

In his husky American twang he said to me, 'You see that guy over there? Well, you know who that is, right?'

'Oh, my God, are you serious? 'Course I know who that is!' I squealed.

'So, you girls wanna party with Drake?'

I stood there, open-mouthed, nodding my head like a Churchill dog. I was so deliriously happy, I could have cried.

'Are you actually fucking serious?' I said to the guy.

'Yeah, girl, you promise me you gonna be cool?' he said, making sure I wasn't going to act like some silly little fan.

'Yeah, course – I was just a little shocked, that's all,' I explained.

He walked me over to the table, along with Erin and Nina. Within seconds, the man of moment passed me a glass of champagne. I remember all this so vividly because I have replayed it in my head a thousand times.

'So, what's your name?' asked Drake.

'Hey, I'm Lateysha,' I said, my hands literally trembling with excitement.

'That's a crazy accent you have! Where are you from?' he said, while looking me up and down with those trademark smouldering eyes.

'I'm from the UK – Wales, actually,' I replied, still trying to disguise my shaky voice and hands. *Just be cool, 'Teesh, just be cool*, I kept telling myself.

'That's cool! We gonna have a good party tonight?'

'Definitely!' I beamed, while Drake, *the* Drake, clinked my glass with his and pecked me on the cheek. At that moment if I'd been struck by a thunderbolt, I would have died happy – I was on Cloud Nine.

I felt like Drake was royalty, in the way that you can't talk to him unless he talks to you, so I wasn't about to start chewing his ear off about his music. I didn't mind, though; I was happy enough just to be in his presence. The drinks were flowing all night – in fact, they were flowing a little too much – and pretty soon, Nina was paralytic. She literally couldn't stand up.

Poor Nina was a lightweight and so battered – I couldn't even get some water down her neck. She grabbed me and said she was going to be sick. The only thing worse than making me leave

Drake's table was being asked to leave by his minders because my friend had barfed all over it! I wasn't going to let that happen in a million years so seconds later, I made the heartbreaking decision to take my friend home and leave before I could talk any more with my favourite rapper.

My Drake dream was over.

It kills me to think of what might have been. Not that I'm saying anything would have gone on between Drake and me, but who knows where the night would have taken us? We could have been best mates! I take solace in the fact that at least I can say I met him and did the right thing in taking my friend home when she needed looking after, but it damn near kills me!

Let's hope we meet again.

Chapter Thirty-two

AMIR KHAN

It was another night out, down South Beach. Erin, Armi and myself had taken a good few hours to get ready and we were looking lush. Nina was staying in that evening, so it was just the three amigos. I'd opted for a skin-tight champagne-gold coloured dress, low-cut to show off my ample assets. I decided to wear my hair down, because now it was ultra-long, I could swish it about. Our new friend Prince had got us a table at one of the hottest clubs, Mansion.

If you've ever been to this super club, you'll know just how iconic and cutting-edge it is. And if not, allow me to explain. You walk into the lobby, which sets the scene for the venue's larger-than-life, expensive interior. I was blown away by the gigantic futuristic chandelier, which hung in the entrance. We strutted into the main room and were gobsmacked by the whole place. The dance floor features a towering LED ceiling, while the DJ box is in the centre of the club so they can be viewed from a 360-degree angle. Everywhere I looked there was different lighting and video screens – it was the coolest place I'd ever been to in my life. I can't do the place justice, so Google it when you get the chance.

As we walked inside the music was thumping, the place was packed and I was instantly up for a good night. Before we sat down, we did our requisite lap of the club to see who was in there. Miami is great for celeb spotting and it's hard to find a night where there's not some A-lister knocking back the Patron.

Sure enough, I spotted someone I recognised. It was the English world champion boxer, Amir Khan. Immediately, I grabbed my friend Erin and pointed in his direction.

'Oh my God, it's Amir Khan!' I whispered to her, excitedly.

'No, it's not,' she insisted, without getting a proper look at him.

'It *is*! I'm sure of it. I'm going to ask him for a picture,' I told her, defiantly.

I strolled up to him like such a groupie and as I approached, I was convinced it must be him.

Amir was sat with his stunning wife, Faryal Makhdoom, when I sheepishly asked him for a photo. She smiled at me with the most perfect white teeth and exotic eyes, and I felt like I had to apologise for interrupting their evening.

'Sorry, but do you mind if we have a picture with him?' I said to her.

'No, it's fine,' she said, while flaring her nostrils. Clearly she was tamping.

Erin took the photo for me (which I have included in this book) and we left them to enjoy their night.

A few hours later, Amir's wife had left the club. No sooner had she walked out the door than Amir made a beeline for our table. Like an eager puppy he bounded towards us (he might as well have had his tongue out). We were just dancing, drinking and having a laugh when he asked to join us. And we were all welcoming girls, so why not?

I was chatting to a few people we had met in the club when my friend Armi went to the bathroom. I noticed Amir followed her and when I asked what had gone on, she told me Amir accosted her outside the toilets and asked her to have sex with him in the disabled cubicle. She had flatly refused (trust me when I say Armi is not that type of girl!) and so they came back to our table.

Next, it was Erin's turn to be propositioned by the pro boxer. Again, he asked her to go to the bathroom, so he could do her quickly in there.

God, he was embarrassing! He had all the class of a cheating footballer. What planet was this guy on? Maybe back in Bolton some tart would give him a shag in the toilets but this was Miami, baby, and the girls here don't do anything like that – at least not unless they're getting a new Hermès or something. To be honest, we all found his desperation hilarious and were just playing him for a fool.

After another hour, we decided to leave the club. We were just saying our goodbyes to Amir when he insisted on joining us wherever we were going. Which I thought was odd: why wasn't he going back to see his wife? In her place I wouldn't have been at all happy. Honestly, I don't know why these guys get married in the first place if all they want to do is mess around with other girls! Can you ever trust anyone these days?

The other girls and me were all starving, so we decided to head to a Mexican restaurant called Peppers, not far from Mansion. Of course, Amir was like a little lost puppy, following us around, and came along for some fajitas. (That's not a euphemism, by the way; we did actually eat some!)

I remember sitting in the restaurant, thinking my whole night was so surreal, just like everything else since I'd got to Miami. There I was, chowing down on some spicy chicken with a world champion boxer and my two best pals. Again, it was a reminder that my life was now a far cry from the Welsh Valleys.

Now, I'll give Amir one thing, he was persistent. No wonder he's such a successful sportsman because he literally never gives up. Over dinner, he kept asking us all if we would have a foursome back at our apartment. He kept saying it like it was no big deal and then making out that we were being difficult. In fact, he got so desperate he even offered us money to go back.

'I'll give you $3,000,' he said, 'a thousand each – that money is nothing to me. Let's go to your apartment now. Come on, I will get you the cash.'

Can you believe it? Who did he think we were, hookers? I was really offended by his comments and looked at him in sheer disgust.

'Excuse me?' I asked, incredulously, 'Let me get this straight, you want to give us money to sleep with you?'

He looked at me sheepishly, but didn't reply.

'Oh, my life! You want to give us money to sleep with you? Ha, ha!' I laughed in his face.

'Aw, is that what you have to do to get a girl? You have to pay them?' I continued in a degrading baby voice. 'Is that how you got your wife?'

Amir's face started to twist with anger.

'Shut up, man! I'm just saying I don't give a fuck about money! I've probably forgot more money than you've ever earned,' he said with venom.

I continued to laugh, but the other girls could sense the tension and calmed the situation down by quickly changing the subject. Even with the offer of cash, we still had zero interest. He couldn't get his head around why we weren't fawning all over him. You could tell he was frustrated because he wasn't getting his own way.

While we were having dinner I slyly took a photo of him and Erin together. I wasn't going to do anything with the photo, I just wanted to keep it to remind me of what a crazy night we'd had, but he saw me take the snap and was absolutely tamping.

He was shouting over the table at me, 'Delete that picture now! Delete it now – my wife will go nuts!'

I continued laughing, saying, 'I'm not going to show anyone, don't worry.'

'That's not the point, delete that picture *now*!' he raged.

'Well then, why are you having dinner with three girls if you have a wife?' I said.

'Delete that picture now, man!' he repeated.

Honestly, I thought he was going to knock ten bells out of me! I've seen him fight too and I didn't want to be on the receiving end of it, so unfortunately I had to delete the picture.

To get him to go away, we said he could come and meet us later at our apartment. Erin had swapped numbers with him earlier in the evening before she realised what a lech he was and unfortunately, she'd told him where we were staying. We just said we would meet him later, but actually had no intention of doing so. He might be a millionaire boxer, but you know what, we just thought he was some weasel perv and craved our beds. We left Amir to pay the bill while we jumped in a cab.

About ten minutes later, we pulled up in a taxi outside our apartment and couldn't believe our eyes: there was Amir in his grey polo T-shirt and jeans, with his phone permanently attached to his ear, looking bewildered. You might have mistaken him for a normal guy, had it not been for his ridiculously gaudy diamond watch. Who knows how he got home before us.

He was standing by the entrance, power ringing Erin's mobile, which she was letting ring out without answering. It was so funny to see how desperate he was to come and meet us. Never in a million years had we expected him to show up at our place.

This kind of guy is just unbelievable. He should have been at home, tucked up in bed with his wife, not trying to party with three girls and looking to get his leg over.

After spotting him outside our apartment block, we made the taxi driver spin round while we all crouched down on the back seat so he couldn't see us. We were literally howling in the taxi, watching him stare at his phone and getting increasingly annoyed that Erin wasn't answering.

Eventually we made our way back up to our apartment through another door without being spotted by him. He must have left soon after, but his persistence never wavered. He kept calling and calling. Erin answered, although it was more so we could laugh at his cringing desperation. He kept asking if we were at home and could he come round and see us, but there was no way. We were done in and quite frankly we'd had enough of him behaving like a dog with two dicks.

Sorry, Amir! Access denied.

The next day, we woke up recounting and laughing about our night. It was just so random, even for us. We couldn't believe how Amir had carried on – telling his wife that she had to go home so he could chat up three girls in a club, then accosting two of us for a quickie, taking us for dinner, offering us money for a foursome and then turning up at our apartment block. What a pathetic, pitiful man he is! I know many girls would have been falling over themselves to get the attention he was lavishing on us, but not us. We genuinely didn't care who he was or what he had achieved in life. To us, he was just another low-life, lying guy who wanted to fuck, and then fuck off back to his missus.

Amir's ears must have been burning because as we were ripping the piss out of him, Erin's phone rang. It came up 'unknown caller', as it had the previous night. Again, out of sheer curiosity, she answered it and listened to what he had to say. I didn't hear the whole conversation, but in a nutshell, he told her he was leaving for the UK in a couple of days' time and could they arrange a date before then? Erin continued to wind up him, saying 'You should have called me earlier, we could have gone for lunch.' Amir sounded disappointed and said that they would hook up back in Manchester, before they said their goodbyes and the conversation ended.

Later that day, I grabbed my iPad and started to check out the latest gossip on the *Mail Online*. I was idly flicking through the right-hand sidebar when up popped a story about our pestering dinner guest from the previous night. The headline read 'Amir Khan relaxes with wife Faryal on the beach in Miami as contender continues to wait for next opponent to be confirmed'. I clicked on the article and scrolled through the photos.

There he was, our mate Amir, baring his champion-winning chest in the sun as his wife wandered behind him on her mobile. I kept thinking about that poor girl and the nonsense she had to put up with. It can't be any kind of life, with all his lies, deceits and devious ways. It made me feel sad for her. Then again, I have read many stories in the press about Amir. From call girls to lap dancers, he's tried to seduce them all in the same way. I've even seen the naked selfies he sent to someone, which then went viral on the Internet and his wife still stayed with him.

Maybe she knows exactly what he's like and turns a blind eye. Who knows?

Chapter Thirty-three

BOOTY CALL

Before I went to Miami, I thought I had a decent body. I'm slim, fairly toned, my boobs are now enormous, thanks to those 34E implants, and my butt was fairly peachy too. But after my first day of seeing a bevvy of bikini-clad beauties on South Beach, I realised I needed to raise my game.

Let me tell you, if you have any body hang-ups, Miami is not the place to go. Every girl is a size zero, with boobs to rival Katie Price, abs like J. Lo and a butt like Beyoncé. Muffin tops and ham arms are not welcome.

Like I said, I was pretty happy with my body but after seeing literally thousands of perfect bottoms, I began to get really depressed and self-conscious about mine. Miami has a Latin flavour, probably because it's so close to South America, which is why everyone has these amazing Brazilian butts. So, how did they achieve this coveted ass shape? Surely they weren't all doing mammoth sessions of squats and lunges?

All the girls who worked at the strip club we always went to had the same gorgeous round arses and the more I kept seeing them, the more I wanted mine to be the same. So, what was their secret? Well, like most things in Miami, everything's available for a price, including a juicy behind.

The strippers gave me the name of the woman they used to plump up their posteriors for the hefty price of $2,400 (roughly £1,500). If I'm honest, I wasn't comfortable spending that amount of money, but this was something I really wanted and who knows, it could help further my modelling career. I started looking on my butt job as an investment.

If you hadn't realised by now after reading this far, I am an impulsive person. I very rarely think about the consequences of my actions until something bad happens. I have a kind of 'just do it, and deal with it later' attitude, which is why I didn't tell many people I was going to have my butt enlarged. As far as I'm concerned it's no one else's decision but mine and I didn't need to ask permission. I was paying for the damn thing. I ran the idea past my boyfriend Ben, who said he was worried for me, but wouldn't ever try and talk me out of doing something I wanted. I told a couple of my girl friends back in Wales too, who were all jealous – they'd been squatting thousands in an attempt to get their own peachy bum.

I made an appointment with a lady called Dr. Jenn*. She gave me the address for a clinic just off Lincoln Avenue, one of the city's most notable streets. Arriving at my appointment a couple of days later, I was beyond excited. The clinic was ultra-modern, with tufted white walls and cool, funky paintings and it was fragranced with stunning white lilies. On the coffee table there were leaflets for all kinds of body and face modifications, from Botox, fillers and 3-D lipo to hair transplants and boob jobs.

I was busy looking at all the 'before' and 'after' photos when Dr. Jenn breezed into the waiting room, with her honey-blonde

---

* Name of the real doctor has been changed

hair and lab coat. Dr. Jenn was, as you might expect, perfect. A bit too perfect, perhaps. Like a Barbie doll whose face was impossibly frozen with a tub full of toxins, but what do you expect when you work in this industry? It's an occupational hazard, I suppose.

She invited me into her treatment room, which again was ultra-swish and modern. Dr. Jenn starting talking to me about the procedure and it was clear from her accent she wasn't from round these parts. She had a strong southern twang, like Dolly Parton. I thought I was going to get my rump pumped right then and there, but this was only a consultation.

Like every American, Dr. Jenn was super-nice and friendly, managing to put me at ease quickly. She made me take off my shorts, leaving just my thong on, so she could see what she had to work with. After telling her what I hoped for and showing her my wish pictures, she agreed the look I was after could be achieved with the use of fillers. She discussed with me how much she was going to use to give my butt the desired volume and I was pleased with everything we talked about. I paid her the money and began to get dressed.

'So, when can I come in for my treatment?' I asked.

'Oh no, ma'am! We come to *you*. Have you got an apartment or hotel room we can come to?' she asked in her Southern drawl.

'Yeah, I'm staying at some apartments near the beach – I can give you the address. But I don't mind coming here,' I said, puzzled.

'That's fine, Mizz Grace, we will come to you. I will book you in for Saturday, three days from now. How's 2pm?'

'Erm, yeah, OK,' I replied, still unsure why she would want to come to my place. It was an absolute bombsite – I'd have to make sure I got the Marigolds out before she came over!

'All righty, Mizz Grace,' she said, beaming as much as her Botox would allow. 'We'll see you then. Have a good day now.'

As I walked out of the clinic I was still bemused as to why she would want to come to my place, but I took solace in the fact that nearly every girl at the club had used her services and their bums looked stunning. Three days from now, I would have the butt of my dreams.

The buzzer went in our apartment and I jumped up with excitement. It was Saturday, the day I was getting my ass plumped, and I genuinely couldn't wait. Of course I was nervous, especially about the pain, but pain is beauty, I reasoned.

I rushed over to open the door, expecting to see the smiley Barbie doll, Dr. Jenn, but I was pretty shocked to see a five-foot Mexican lady wearing a dentist's white coat and carrying a metal briefcase instead.

'Oh, hi. Are you with Dr. Jenn?' I asked.

'Sí, Señora,' she answered, barging her way through the door.

'Is she on her way up or...' I said, thinking this lady must have been employed to carry the equipment.

'No, just me,' she replied.

In broken English she somehow managed to tell me that she performed the injections for Dr. Jenn. She then motioned for me to lie face down on my bed, with nothing on my bottom half.

I was instantly unsure. Suddenly I didn't feel good about this treatment and began wanting to back out. But if I backed out now, I would lose all my money and still not have the bum I so badly wanted. If I wasn't feeling nervous before, I definitely was now. Where was Dr. Jenn?

I regretted not asking more questions in the consultation. Like, are you going to be performing these injections? What filler will you use? Why do I have to have this done at my apartment? Is it actually legal? And probably, most importantly, is it safe? I felt sick to the core. At the time, only my friend Erin was in the apartment with me, and she was simply curious as to how my butt would look because she was thinking of having it done herself. My other two friends had made themselves scarce and decided to top up their tans on the beach.

The lady grabbed a stool I used to do my make-up on and set up her 'operating tools'. She opened her briefcase and pulled out four huge needles and four syringes. I saw a clear liquid gel in two containers, which she lined up.

I crossed my fingers as I lay down on the bed and buried my face in a pillow, hoping this was going to be OK.

First, she rubbed anaesthetic cream all over my bum and let that work its magic for a few minutes. I'd had this kind of cream before when I had my lips done – it takes away the pain of the needle piercing the skin, but not the pain of the actual stuff being injected. I began to sweat just thinking about what would happen next.

'Ready?' she grunted.

I closed my eyes and took a deep breath.

'Yeah, I'm ready,' I said and tensed my whole body, waiting for that first stab of pain to hit me.

The prick of the needle was a piece of cake because I'd had the numbing cream, but as she slid the needle deeper into my layers of tissue, a searing pain shot through my body.

'FUCKING HELL!' I screamed, as I felt the weird sensation of the liquid gel filtering into my left cheek. 'OH MY FUCKING GOD!' I yelled, as I bit down on the pillow.

The woman administering this agony didn't flinch for a second and I remember thinking she must be used to people reacting like this. Surely this should be done with a local anaesthetic?

Tears instantly filled my eyes as she continued to empty the syringe into me. It was the worst pain I've ever felt in my life. Worse than the time I had 'Valleywood' tattooed on my foof.

'OK?' she asked, as she tossed one needle into her box.

'Oh my God, no! This hurts so much,' I said, sniffling.

'Other side,' she told me, as she slapped my right butt cheek.

I knew the pain was coming any second now and my whole body just froze. All the while I kept thinking about all kinds to take my mind off the intense ache, but as soon as I felt the penetration again, my thoughts just emptied and all I could focus on was this fire erupting in my arse cheek.

'OH, FUCKKKK!' I screamed again as the second syringe was blasted into me. I could barely breathe. It didn't help that the woman, this demon sent from hell, didn't speak a word of the Queen's and couldn't do anything to explain what was happening and soothe my suffering.

I squealed all the way through until she had emptied the second syringe into me.

Afterwards, I lifted my head up and turned around to look at my poor bum, which was in excruciating pain. It didn't even look any fuller, which was so discouraging.

'Ready?' she asked again, as she knifed another needle into me on my left side, slightly higher than the last injection. I was hoping my natural adrenalin would kick in and stop this agony, but it never got any easier.

I could feel the blood trickling down my ass when she pulled out the needle, letting it spill on my white duvet cover. The sight of it made me want to vomit.

'Last one,' she laughed, as she stabbed the final injection into me.

'FUCKING HELL!' I shrieked, squeezing my pillow as hard as I possibly could, until after a few seconds the ordeal was over.

She began massaging my bum and rolling the gel in between her fingers to even it out. I can't tell you how sore I was – the pain was deep down into my ass. I didn't know how I would ever sit down again, anytime soon.

After a few minutes of massaging, she rose and said, 'We done!' She then unravelled a load of kitchen roll, yes, KITCHEN ROLL, and wound it around my wounds as if it were bandages. Why she didn't use actual bandages is beyond me.

She packed up her briefcase, handed me a printout of do's and don'ts and promptly left.

Immediately, I ran over to the mirror to take a look at my new booty. Yeah, it was bigger and more projected, just as I had wanted. I spun round to look at it from all angles and I was really pleased with the results. The only downside was the pain, which was horrendous: my whole butt was literally on fire.

On the printout she gave me it said that I couldn't sit down for twenty-four hours, I couldn't wear tight clothing, no hot baths or showers, and to stay in and relax. If the pain became unbearable, I was to take painkillers, but she didn't give me any antibiotics.

I spent the next day and night sat in my knickers, watching films with Erin and watching fluid leak out of my stab wounds, which was absolutely gross. With hindsight, I wish I had carried out more research, but it was done now and I just had to hope for the best.

So what exactly did I actually have injected into me? The truth is, I'm not quite sure but my guess would be a filler called Hydrogel; basically, industrial-strength silicone. And the reason the procedure was done at my apartment was because these injections are illegal and not approved by the FDA. Administering injections of this sort by a non-licensed professional is also against the law, not only in America but also in the UK.

Great news, huh? I kept dreaming about my bum suddenly

giving me gangrene or some of the silicone seeping out into my bloodstream. It made me wish I'd never had the procedure done.

Honestly, I'm such a foolish risk-taker sometimes. After googling the procedure, up came all sorts of horror stories of people who had died because of this treatment. I just had to hope everything was going to be OK and my 'tush didn't turn toxic, or I didn't know what I would do.

Most certainly, I didn't want to be leaving Miami in a body bag.

I had my injections in September 2014, and at the time of writing this book, I'm pleased to say I've had absolutely no problems and was recovered almost fully after about a week. I know I was stupid not to do my research and if I could give any advice, it would be to know everything about what you are about to do. Don't put your life in danger – it's just not worth it.

It's crazy to think that ten years ago everyone wanted boobs like Pamela Anderson. Now, it's all about the booty, thanks to Kim Kardashian, Nicki Minaj and Jennifer Lopez. So I understand the appeal of wanting a bigger behind, but also that it's just a trend. In no way, shape or form do I advocate getting your bum made bigger, but if you insist on going down that road use a licensed professional and a well-known safe product. Or here's an idea, and one I should have thought of myself – why not get off your bum and do some squats? Yeah, it will take time to build the booty of your dreams, but it will be so natural and safe and no one can ever take that away from you.

You can be proud of a peach produced through nothing but blood, sweat and tears.

EPILOGUE

Well, that's almost a wrap from me! I hope you've enjoyed reading about the highs and lows of my life in *Valleywood*, but my story isn't finished yet and who knows what will get thrown at me next?

I've been through some tough times in my twenty-two years. It all happened and yet I'm still here, with a smile on my face and hope in my heart.

Writing this book has been a real trip down memory lane. Often, when I thought about some of the more turbulent times, I would become upset because for years I've tried to block out the stuff that was too painful to think about. Dragging it all up again in order to share my life story has been, at times, unbelievably distressing. Nevertheless, it was important for me to share it with you, because like I said at the very beginning, I was only going to write this 'warts and all' account of my life if I could say what I wanted, how I wanted and in the way I wanted.

Sometimes I can't believe I'm the same girl who was once so

badly depressed I almost took my own life, because now I look in the mirror and see a strong, capable, powerful young woman. And I don't mean that in an arrogant way, I just mean I've been through a lot and managed to come out the other side a better person.

Many times I could have gone off the rails when I was younger and blamed it on my upbringing. I could have just moaned about the cards I'd been dealt in life and put up with my situation, but I'm not my circumstances. I wanted a better life than the one my mother had, so I've put myself out there and grabbed every opportunity that has come my way. Let that be a lesson to you all: take the first opportunity you can, while you can, because you may never be dealt a second one.

Right now, I'm back tearing up Miami, while building contacts for the future. The last time I was out here, I met many influential people who are now helping me with my modelling and TV career. I hope to be back on screen again soon and I'm still working on my music. And if all else fails, I suppose I could take those pole-dancing lessons more seriously!

I've said a few times during the course of this book that my mum and me have had some rocky times. We had a very cold, distant, unaffectionate relationship but I'm glad to say that slowly we are building on becoming closer. In fact, these days we get on really well and I love her so much, which is why I've dedicated this book to her. She is – believe it or not – the strongest woman I know. My word, she's been through a lot and she's still here with a smile on her face. I know she is unbelievably proud of me and everything I have achieved and I'm going to continue to work really hard so that I can treat her to a better life. A life she deserves after being through so much trauma for years.

Regan and me still have that most special unbreakable bond

and I am so proud of the man he has become. I couldn't ask for a better brother, I am truly blessed to have him in my life. We have been through so much together and we have always had each other's back. Even though he is eighteen now and finally taller than me, I still want to look after him and protect him. I love him more than all the weaves in the world.

My other siblings, Paris, Kason and Madison, all mean the world to me too. Paris is beyond stunning; how she is not a top model by now I'll never know. She is the sweetest, kindest girl and I know she is going to be an amazing young woman. Kason will always be like a son to me. Ever since he was born I felt so protective of him and I know I always will. I really want the best for him in life and if I can help in any way I will because I love him dearly. My mini Madison is growing up so fast too, but she's still small enough to sit on my knee. I love her because she is so innocent and I want her to stay that way as long as possible. I know I grew up too fast, perhaps because I had all my other siblings to worry about, but she doesn't and I hope she relishes the fact she's the baby of the bunch.

I don't know what the future holds for me, but I'm happy not knowing. I want to travel the world, see all there is to see and experience everything from the Amazon rainforests to the peak of Kilimanjaro and beyond. Seriously, I want to do it all!

Most have me pegged as a diva, but I hope by now you know me a little better – you will have seen a different side to me. Only the other month, I was enquiring about volunteering at an orphanage in Africa, something a lot of people might be shocked to learn. They think I'm too wrapped up my own plastic, superficial world to care about the less fortunate, which is not the case at all. Deep down, I'm a truly selfless, caring person and someday soon, I would love to be able to help in any small way

I want to broaden my horizons and then maybe start a family of my own. I'm really happy with my boyfriend Ben and in the next few years I would love for us to have a baby together, but I'm not going to put any pressure on myself just yet. For now, I'm taking life by the scruff of the neck and enjoying everything that comes my way.

Ten years from now, I want to look back and see the life I chose, not the one I had to settle for.

If you take nothing else from this book, take this:

Don't let hard lessons harden your heart.
Forget the past.
Live in the present and let the future take care of itself.

All my love,
Lateysha. x

THANK YOU

I want to thank everyone who has helped me put this book together, it's not been an easy task to say the least, but I really appreciate everyone's hard work and dedication in helping me tell my story.

I would firstly like to say a huge thank you to my amazing ghost writer Elissa Corrigan. It was emotionally draining talking about my difficult past but she managed to put me at ease and made it easier to discuss some of the more turbulent years. She's worked her ass off on this book and I think she deserves a lot of credit for all her hard work, patience and understanding. Love you. X.

To my brother Regan, thanks for always standing by me no matter what. He's recently signed for St. Helens rugby team and I couldn't be happier for him. I've watched him grow from a little boy into a man and he will always be my number one. You make me the proudest sister in the world.

To my agent Luke and his team at Misfits Celebrity management – Alex, Christy and Adam – I don't know where I would be without all of you. You are always on the other end of the phone whenever I need advice or help and I can't thank you all enough. Luke, you spotted something in me years ago when no one else wanted to know and for that I will be eternally grateful. I seriously don't know where I'd be without you. You push me to my limits, work hard on my behalf and put up with my diva strops. You guys are the best.

Erin, you are like a sister to me. A soul sister. We have had some crazy times together and I'm looking forward to making so many more memories.

Harrison, Casey, Ellis and Niamh, thank you for being there for me through thick and thin. You are truly amazing friends and I'm so blessed to have all of you in my life. Whether I was broke or rich, you would always treat me exactly the same way and you would always be there with me until the end. True friendship never dies.

Roberta Duman, Head of Publicity for MTV. You've been a total babe. Seriously I can't thank you enough for pushing me and always looking out for me even when I was being a total pain.

The wider MTV Publicity Team: Hayley Hamburg; Jade Reuben; Lauren Goddard. I know how hard you all work behind the scenes and I'm very grateful.

The now departed Natasha Lewis. I've missed you so much since you left, Tash. You had the most impossible job ever managing all of *The Valleys* and *Geordie Shore* cast and I'll never know how you did it. Sorry for every time I've been short or upset down the phone and best of luck in Australia.

Steve Regan, the man who created *The Valleys*. It was all your idea to start with Steve and what an idea it was! I'm so happy that even though the show has ended for now with MTV that you're forever my friend. Do you remember when I was temporarily homeless and you offered to let me move in? I love you very much.

Also to Craig Orr who works with Steve. It's your skill and

creativity that helped tame us reckless kids into an amazing TV show. Thanks Craig.

The MTV bosses who I've heard mentioned so many times but I rarely get to meet. Kerry Taylor the MTV UK General Manager. It was your faith in *The Valleys* that got it on to screens, so I thank you for the opportunity. Rebecca Knight, Head of Production, I know you spent many hours working behind the scenes to make the numbers work and help us making a living so thank you, Rebecca. Jo Bacon, I know you were involved with the show right from the beginning and helped to make the show such a huge success on social media, so thanks again.

Everyone else at MTV – everyone in legal, finance, digital media, social, editing, marketing and press. You all do such an amazing job.

As you've read throughout this book, True North make the show for MTV and in charge is Fiona O'Sullivan. Fiona, you're actually like an inspiration to me. You're such a powerful and professional woman and I'd love to achieve what you have some day. Thank you for working around the clock to make this TV show what it became. You're dedication and resolve have been key and I'll never forget that.

Series Producer of *The Valleys*, Manus 'Leprechaun' Wynne. Manus you spent a lot of hours on the ground with all the cast, and had to physically make the show work. You've been such a kind and caring person even when I spent weeks making things difficult for you. I always called you 'the Devil' but really you're an angel. Thank you.

Everyone else at True North who put their life on hold to make *The Valleys* including Nat Grant, Liz Foley, Steve McConville, Fay Gibson, Hetal Dhanak, Dan McGowan, Emma Cowley, Jonny Dixon, Daniel Lewis, Matt Andrews, Gareth Prosser, Jay Ahmed,

John Newman, Rose Hibbot, Mark Littlewood, Illona Burton, Finn Furlong, Ainsley, Dinkesh, Daisy and Jarrek.

The team at Big Bang who work with my management booking Pas. Thank you to Yusef, Liz, Tanee, Ashley, Steve and Karol. I had a lot of fun at my PAs.

There's a lot of people in the press I owe thanks to. Thank you Jen Crothers, Natasha Rigler, Damien McSorley, Sam Riley, Matt Beadle, Jeany Savage, Nadine Linge, Dan Wootton and Leigh Holmwood.

I'd like to thank some commercial partners I've worked with including Mike at LoveSasha, Dukes and the gorge Sophia May, Paul Dudbridge, Paulien Bolhaar and everyone else.

A HUGE thank you to John Blake Publishing, who went through a lot of work to publish this book. Thanks to John himself, Chris, Joanna and everyone else at the team who have done such an amazing job. I hope you're as proud as I am with what we've achieved.

Thank you to the hero that is Dr Miles Berry. Dr Berry helped transform my life with a breast augmentation. It's not an overstatement to say Dr Berry, in my opinion, is the best surgeon in the world; your extraordinary skills are only matched by your caring personality. Also to Teresa from Love London PR for helping to arrange everything.

There's a couple of famous faces to thank including the cast of *The Valleys*. Natalee Harris, Aron Williams, Carley Belmonte, Darren Chidgey, Jenna Jonathan, Leeroy Reed, Liam Powell, Nicole Morris, Jason & Anthony Suminski, Jack Watkins, AK and Jordan. I love each and every one of you.

Thank you to the beautiful Holly Hagan from *Geordie Shore*. We share the same management and you've always been on hand for girl-talk and advice. You're a really lovely girl and I'm thankful for our friendship. The same for Marnie Simpson, also from *Geordie Shore*.